To Liz —
From Mrs. Samore, June '99

Latino Literature

PRENTICE HALL
Upper Saddle River, New Jersey
Needham, Massachusetts

ISBN 0-13-435445-1

1 2 3 4 5 6 7 8 9 10   02 01 00 99 98

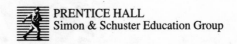

PRENTICE HALL
Simon & Schuster Education Group

Acknowledgments

Grateful acknowledgment is made to the following for copyrighted material:

Teresa Paloma Acosta

"Family Story for your Twenty-First Birthday" by Teresa Paloma Acosta.

Addison-Wesley

"A Shot At It" from *When I Was Puerto Rican* by Esmeralda Santiago. Copyright © 1993 by Esmeralda Santiago.

Arte Publico Press

"A Voice" from *Communion* by Pat Mora. Copyright © 1991 Pat Mora. (Arte Publico Press, University of Houston, 1991). "Immigrants" from *Borders* by Pat Mora. Copyright © 1986 by Pat Mora. (Arte Publico Press, University of Houston, 1986). "Elena" from *Chants* by Pat Mora. Copyright © 1985 by Pat Mora. (Arte Publico Press, University of Houston, 1985). All rights reserved. "Distillation," by Hugo Martínez-Serros, published in an earlier version in *Chicago*, October 1980, from *The Last Laugh and Other Stories* by Hugo Martínez-Serros. Copyright © 1988 by Hugo Martínez-Serros. (Houston: Arte Publico Press-University of Houston, 1988). "Lessons of Love" from *Silent Dancing: A Partial Remembrance of a Puerto Rican Childhood* by Judith Ortiz Cofer. Copyright © 1990 Judith Ortiz Cofer. (Arte Publico Press, University of Houston, 1990). "Which Line Is This? I Forget" by Lorna Dee Cervantes, from *Kikiriki, Stories and Poems in English and Spanish for Children*, edited by Sylvia Cavazos Peña, 1981. (Houston: Arte Publico Press-University of Houston, 1981). "The Latin Deli" by Judith Ortiz Cofer, and "Sweet Drama" by Luis Omar Salinas from *Decade II: An Anniversary Anthology*, edited by Julian Olivares and Evangelina Vigil-Pinon. Copyright © 1993.

(Acknowledgments continue on p. 126.)

Contents

Introduction

The purpose of this anthology is to collect in one book works by outstanding Latino writers that are representative of their vibrant cultures. The selections in this collection illustrate the cultural wealth gained from the Latino community and the contributions made to the literary history of the United States.

Although this anthology groups the work of these prominent Latino writers into different genres—short stories and folk tales, nonfiction, and poetry—the selections share common themes, such as deep family ties, cultural confusion, the challenges of language and cultural barriers, and growing up. The various genres bring these issues to us in the form of imaginative stories, magical folk tales, riveting personal experiences, intelligent commentary, and the musical language of poetry.

Many of the selections in this anthology focus on the challenges families face of becoming "Americanized" while attempting to retain their native cultures. The short stories of Julia Alvarez and Hugo Martínez-Serros and the poetry of Teresa Paloma Acosta, Francisco X. Alarcón, and Luis Omar Salinas celebrate the bonds created by the love of parents and grandparents and the comforts and protection provided by these relationships. The pride a mother feels about her daughter in Alvarez's short story is comparable to Sandra Cisneros's memory of her father's pride in her accomplishments in "Only Daughter." Another type of family bond presents itself in Judith Ortiz Cofer's short story in which a young boy becomes intrigued by the mysteries of his grandfather and longs to know more about him.

The longing to become more in tune with the primary culture of one's ancestor is also the subject of Martín Espada's poem "We Live by What We See at Night," where Espada tries to imagine his father's homeland. Cultural confusion that interferes with the establishment of identity is the theme of Lorna Dee Cervantes's and William Carlos Williams's poetry. This confusion also manifests in a longing for the comforts of one's native culture, as described in Judith Ortiz Cofer's poem "The Latin Deli: Ars Poetica" and Martín Espada's "Tony Went to the Bodega but He Didn't Buy Anything." The feelings of alienation from one's heritage and the cultural confusion of belonging to two cultures are also a result of the language barriers.

The language problems caused by speaking Spanish at home and hearing English spoken in school are a theme in many Latino works. Pat Mora's poem "Elena" tells the story of a mother who wants to learn English because she feels alienated from her English-speaking children. Richard Rodriguez fondly recalls his family's attempt to learn English and how the common struggle drew them closer. In support of retaining one's native language, journalist Carlos Alberto Montaner reassures us about speaking Spanish as well as English in his essay "Why Fear Spanish?"

Other writers deal with issues in the Latino community such as the condition of being an immigrant in a new country. In her poem "Immigrants," Pat Mora describes the hopes for a better life that all immigrants have for their children. Gary Soto's "Field Poem," Sandra Cisneros's short story "Geraldo No Last Name," and Judith Ortiz Cofer's "American History" are less hopeful depictions of the lives of Hispanic immigrants.

Many of the selections in this anthology rejoice in universal experiences as well as in recounting those that are more painful. Nicholasa Mohr's "Mr. Mendelsohn" shows how the kindness of a family changes a lonely man's life. Aurora Levins Morales's poetry and Esmeralda Santiago's autobiography explore strength and courage in the face of what appears to be unbeatable odds. Judith Ortiz Cofer's and Gary Soto's autobiographical pieces explore the innocence and awkwardness of adolescent love, while the poetry of Jimmy Santiago Baca deals with the unselfishness of mature love.

Finally, this anthology includes examples of the rich heritage of the Hispanic peoples. The Spanish folk tales retold by Rudolfo A. Anaya and José Griego y Maestas and those by Ricardo E. Alegría explore cultural values about trust, wealth, honesty, and luck. The magic of these folk tales is present in all the literature of this anthology. Each piece of culturally rich Latino literature helps to weave the tapestry that is America.

Daughter of Invention

Julia Alvarez

SHE wanted to invent something, my mother. There was a period after we arrived in this country, until five or so years later, when my mother was inventing. They were never pressing, global needs she was addressing with her pencil and pad. She would have said that was for men to do, rockets and engines that ran on gasoline and turned the wheels of the world. She was just fussing with little house things, don't mind her.

She always invented at night, after settling her house down. On his side of the bed my father would be conked out for an hour already, his Spanish newspaper draped over his chest, his glasses, propped up on his bedside table, looking out eerily at the darkened room like a disembodied guard. But in her lighted corner, like some devoted scholar burning the midnight oil, my mother was inventing, sheets pulled to her lap, pillows propped up behind her, her reading glasses riding the bridge of her nose like a schoolmarm's. On her lap lay one of those innumerable pads of paper my father always brought home from his office, compliments of some pharmaceutical company, advertising tranquilizers or antibiotics or skin cream; in her other hand, my mother held a pencil that looked like a pen with a little cylinder of lead inside. She would work on a sketch of something familiar, but drawn at such close range so she could attach a special nozzle or handier handle, the thing looked peculiar. Once, I mistook the spiral of a corkscrew for a nautilus shell, but it could just as well have been a galaxy forming.

It was the only time all day we'd catch her sitting down, for she herself was living proof of the *perpetuum mobile* machine so many inventors had sought over the ages. My sisters and I would seek her out now when she seemed to have a moment to talk to us: We were having trouble at school or we wanted her to persuade my father to give us permission to go into the city or to a shopping mall or a movie—in broad daylight! My mother would wave us out of her room. "The problem with you girls . . ." I can tell you right now what the problem always boiled down to: We wanted to become Americans and my father—and my mother, at first—would have none of it.

"You girls are going to drive me crazy!" She always threatened if we kept nagging. "When I end up in Bellevue, you'll be safely sorry!"

She spoke in English when she argued with us, even though, in a matter of months, her daughters were the fluent ones. Her English was much better than my father's, but it was still a mishmash of mixed-up idioms and sayings that showed she was "green behind the ears," as she called it.

If my sisters and I tried to get her to talk in Spanish, she'd snap, "When in Rome, do unto the Romans . . ."

I had become the spokesman for my sisters, and I would stand my ground in that bedroom. "We're not going to that school anymore, Mami!"

"You have to." Her eyes would widen with worry. "In this country, it is against the law not to go to school. You want us to get thrown out?"

"You want us to get killed? Those kids were throwing stones today!"

"Sticks and stones don't break bones . . ." she chanted. I could tell, though, by the look on her face, it was as if one of those stones the kids had aimed at us had hit her. But she always pretended we were at fault. "What did you do to provoke them? It takes two to tangle, you know."

"Thanks, thanks a lot, Mom!" I'd storm out of that room and into mine. I never called her *Mom* except when I wanted her to feel how much she had failed us in this country. She was a good enough Mami, fussing and scolding and giving advice, but a terrible girlfriend parent, a real failure of a Mom.

Back she'd go to her pencil and pad, scribbling and tsking and tearing off paper, finally giving up, and taking up her *New York Times.* Some nights, though, she'd get a good idea, and she'd rush into my room, a flushed look on her face, her tablet of paper in her hand, a cursory knock on the door she'd just thrown open: "Do I have something to show you, Cukita!"

This was my time to myself, after I'd finished my homework, while my sisters were still downstairs watching TV in the basement. Hunched over my small desk, the overhead light turned off, my lamp shining poignantly on my paper, the rest of the room in warm, soft, uncreated darkness, I wrote my secret poems in my new language.

"You're going to ruin your eyes!" My mother would storm into my room, turning on the overly bright overhead light, scaring off whatever shy passion I had just begun coaxing out of a labyrinth of feelings with the blue thread of my writing.

"Oh Mami!" I'd cry out, my eyes blinking up at her. "I'm writing."

"Ay, Cukita." That was her communal pet name for whoever was in her favor. "Cukita, when I make a million, I'll buy you your very own typewriter." (I'd been nagging my mother for one just like the one father had bought her to do his order forms at home.) "Gravy on the turkey" was what she called it when someone was buttering her up. She'd butter and pour. "I'll hire you your very own typist."

Down she'd plop on my bed and hold out her pad to me. "Take a guess, Cukita?" I'd study her rough sketch a moment: soap sprayed from the nozzle head of a shower when you turned the knob a certain way? Coffee with creamer already mixed in? Time-released water capsules for your plants when you were away? A key chain with a timer that would go off when your parking meter was about to expire? (The ticking would help you find your keys easily if you mislaid them.) The famous one, famous only in hindsight, was the stick person dragging a square by a rope—a suitcase with wheels? "Oh, of course," we'd humor her. "What every household needs: a shower like a car wash, keys ticking like a bomb, luggage on a leash!" By now, as you can see, it'd become something of a family joke, our Thomas Edison Mami, our Benjamin Franklin Mom.

Her face would fall. "Come on now! Use your head." One more wrong guess, and she'd tell me, pressing with her pencil point the different highlights of this incredible new wonder. "Remember that time we took the car to Bear Mountain, and we re-ah-lized that we had forgotten to pack an opener with our pick-a-nick?" (We kept correcting her, but she insisted this is how it should be said.) "When we were ready to eat we didn't have any way to open the refreshments cans?" (This before fliptop lids, which she claimed had crossed her mind.) "You know what this is now?" A shake of my head. "Is a car bumper, but see this part is a removable can opener. So simple and yet so necessary, no?"

"Yeah, Mami. You should patent it." I'd shrug. She'd tear off the scratch paper and fold it, carefully, corner to corner, as if she were going to save it. But then, she'd toss it in the wastebasket on her way out of the room and give a little laugh like a disclaimer. "It's half of one or two dozen of another . . ."

I suppose none of her daughters was very encouraging. We resented her spending time on those dumb inventions. Here, we were trying to fit in America among Americans; we needed help figuring out who we were, why these Irish kids whose grandparents were micks two generations ago, why they were calling us spics. Why had we come to the country in the first place? Important, crucial, final things, you see, and here was our own mother, who didn't have a second to help us puzzle any of this out, inventing gadgets to make life easier for American moms. Why, it seemed as if she were arming our own enemy against us!

One time, she did have a moment of triumph. Every night, she liked to read *The New York Times* in bed before turning off her light, to see what the Americans were up to. One night, she let out a yelp to wake up my father beside her, bolt upright, reaching for his glasses which, in his haste, he knocked across the room. *"Que pasa? Que pasa?"* What is wrong? There was terror in his voice, fear she'd seen in his eyes in the Dominican Republic before we left. We were being watched there; he was being followed; he and mother had often exchanged those looks. They could not talk, of course, though they must have whispered to each other in fear at night in the dark bed. Now in America, he was safe, a success even; his Centro Medico in Brooklyn was thronged with the sick and the homesick. But in dreams, he went back to those awful days and long nights, and my mother's screams confirmed his secret fear: We had not gotten away after all; they had come for us at last.

"Ay, Papi, I'm sorry. Go back to sleep, Cukito. It's nothing, nothing really." My mother held up the *Times* for him to squint at the small print, back page headline, one hand tapping all over the top of the bedside table for his glasses, the other rubbing his eyes to wakefulness.

"Remember, remember how I showed you that suitcase with little wheels so we would not have to carry those heavy bags when we traveled? Someone stole my idea and made a million!" She shook the paper in his face. She shook the paper in all our faces that night. "See! See! This man was no *bobo*. He didn't put all his pokers on a back burner. I kept telling you, one of these days my ship would pass me by in the night!" She wagged her finger at my sisters and my father and me, laughing all the while, one of those eerie laughs crazy people in movies laugh. We had congregated in her room to hear the good news she'd been yelling down the stairs, and now we eyed her and each other. I suppose we were all thinking the same thing: Wouldn't it be weird and sad if Mami did end up in Bellevue as she'd always threatened she might?

"*Ya, ya!* Enough!" She waved us out of her room at last. "There is no use trying to drink spilt milk, that's for sure."

It was the suitcase rollers that stopped my mother's hand; she had weather vaned a minor brainstorm. She would have to start taking herself seriously. That blocked the free play of her ingenuity. Besides, she had also begun working at my father's office, and at night, she was too tired and busy filling in columns with how much money they had made that day to be fooling with gadgets!

She did take up her pencil and pad one last time to help me out. In ninth grade, I was chosen by my English teacher, Sister Mary Joseph, to deliver the teacher's day address at the school assembly. Back in the Dominican Republic, I was a terrible student. No one could ever get me to sit down to a book. But in New York, I needed to settle somewhere, and the natives were unfriendly, the country inhospitable, so I took root in the language. By high school, the nuns were reading my stories and compositions out loud to my classmates as examples of imagination at work.

This time my imagination jammed. At first I didn't want and then I couldn't seem to write that speech. I suppose I should have thought of it as a "great honor," as my father called it. But I was mortified. I still had a pronounced lilt to my accent, and I did not like to speak in public, subjecting myself to my classmates' ridicule. Recently, they had begun to warm toward my sisters and me, and it took no great figuring to see that to deliver a eulogy for a convent full of crazy, old overweight nuns was no way to endear myself to the members of my class.

But I didn't know how to get out of it. Week after week, I'd sit down, hoping to polish off some quick, noncommittal little speech. I couldn't get anything down.

The weekend before our Monday morning assembly I went into a panic. My mother would just have to call in and say I was in the hospital, in a coma. I was in the Dominican Republic. Yeah, that was it! Recently, my father had been talking about going back home to live.

My mother tried to calm me down. "Just remember how Mister Lincoln couldn't think of anything to say at the Gettysburg, but then, Bang! 'Four score and once upon a time ago,'" she began reciting. Her version of history was half invention and half truths and whatever else she needed to prove a point. "Something is going to come if you just relax. You'll see, like the

Americans say, 'Necessity is the daughter of invention.' I'll help you."

All weekend, she kept coming into my room with help. "Please, Mami, just leave me alone, please," I pleaded with her. But I'd get rid of the goose only to have to contend with the gander. My father kept poking his head in the door just to see if I had "fulfilled my obligations," a phrase he'd used when we were a little younger, and he'd check to see whether we had gone to the bathroom before a car trip. Several times that weekend around the supper table, he'd recite his valedictorian speech from when he graduated from high school. He'd give me pointers on delivery, on the great orators and their tricks. (Humbleness and praise and falling silent with great emotion were his favorites.)

My mother sat across the table, the only one who seemed to be listening to him. My sisters and I were forgetting a lot of our Spanish, and my father's formal, florid diction was even harder to understand. But my mother smiled softly to herself, and turned the Lazy Susan at the center of the table around and around as if it were the prime mover, the first gear of attention.

That Sunday evening, I was reading some poetry to get myself inspired: Whitman in an old book with an engraved cover my father had picked up in a thrift shop next to his office a few weeks back. "I celebrate myself and sing myself . . ." "He most honors my style who learns under it to destroy the teacher." The poet's words shocked and thrilled me. I had gotten used to the nuns, a literature of appropriate sentiments, poems with a message, expurgated texts. But here was a flesh and blood man, belching and laughing and sweating in poems. "Who touches this book touches a man."

That night, at last, I started to write, recklessly, three, five pages, looking up once only to see my father passing by the hall on tiptoe. When I was done, I read over my words, and my eyes filled. I finally sounded like myself in English!

As soon as I had finished that first draft, I called my mother to my room. She listened attentively, as she had to my father's speech, and in the end, her eyes were glistening too. Her face was soft and warm and proud. "That is a beautiful, beautiful speech, Cukita. I want for your father to hear it before he goes to sleep. Then I will type it for you, all right?"

Down the hall we went, the two of us, faces flushed with accomplishment. Into the master bedroom where my father was propped up on his pillows, still awake, reading the Dominican papers, already days old. He had become interested in his country's fate again. The dictatorship had been toppled. The interim government was going to hold the first free elections in thirty years. There was still some question in his mind whether or not we might want to move back. History was in the making, freedom and hope were in the air again! But my mother had gotten used to the life here. She did not want to go back to the old country where she was only a wife and a mother (and a failed one at that, since she had never had the required son). She did not come straight out and disagree with my father's plans. Instead, she fussed with him about reading the papers in bed, soiling those sheets with those poorly printed, foreign tabloids. "*The Times* is not that bad!" she'd claim if my father tried to humor her by saying they shared the same dirty habit.

The minute my father saw my mother and me, filing in, he put his paper down, and his face brightened as if at long last his wife had delivered a son, and that was the news we were bringing him. His teeth were already grinning from the glass of water next to his bedside lamp, so he lisped when he said, "Eh-speech, eh-speech!"

"It is so beautiful, Papi," my mother previewed him, turning the sound off on his TV. She sat down at the foot of the bed. I stood before both of them, blocking their view of the soldiers in helicopters landing amid silenced gun reports and explosions. A few weeks ago it had been the shores of the Dominican Republic. Now it was the jungles of Southeast Asia they were saving. My mother gave me the nod to begin reading.

I didn't need much encouragement. I put my nose to the fire, as my mother would have said, and read from start to finish without looking up. When I was done, I was a little embarrassed at my pride in my own words. I pretended to quibble with a phrase or two I was sure I'd be talked out of changing. I looked questioningly to my mother. Her face was radiant. She turned to share her pride with my father.

But the expression on his face shocked us both. His toothless mouth had collapsed into a dark zero. His eyes glared at me, then shifted to my mother, accusingly. In barely audible Spanish, as if secret microphones or informers were all about, he whispered, "You will permit her to read *that*?"

My mother's eyebrows shot up, her mouth fell open. In the old country, any whisper of a challenge to authority could bring the secret police in their black V.W.'s. But this was America.

People could say what they thought. "What is wrong with her speech?" my mother questioned him.

"What ees wrrrong with her eh-speech?" My father wagged his head at her. His anger was always more frightening in his broken English. As if he had mutilated the language in his fury—and now there was nothing to stand between us and his raw, dumb anger. "What is wrong? I will tell you what is wrong. It shows no gratitude. It is boastful. 'I celebrate myself'? 'The best student learns to destroy the teacher'?" He mocked my plagiarized words. "That is insubordinate. It is improper. It is disrespecting of her teachers—" In his anger he had forgotten his fear of lurking spies: Each wrong he voiced was a decibel higher than the last outrage. Finally, he was yelling at me, "As your father, I forbid you to say that eh-speech!"

My mother leapt to her feet, a sign always that she was about to make a speech or deliver an ultimatum. She was a small woman, and she spoke all her pronouncements standing up, either for more protection or as a carry-over from her girlhood in convent schools where one asked for, and literally took, the floor in order to speak. She stood by my side, shoulder to shoulder; we looked down at my father. "That is no tone of voice, Eduardo—" she began.

By now, my father was truly furious. I suppose it was bad enough I was rebelling, but here was my mother joining forces with me. Soon he would be surrounded by a house full of independent American women. He too leapt from his bed, throwing off his covers. The Spanish newspapers flew across the room. He snatched my speech out of my hands, held it before my panicked eyes, a vengeful, mad look in his own, and then once, twice, three, four, countless times, he tore my prize into shreds.

"Are you crazy?" My mother lunged at him. "Have you gone mad? That is her speech for tomorrow you have torn up!"

"Have *you* gone mad?" He shook her away. "You were going to let her read that . . . that insult to her teachers?"

"Insult to her teachers!" My mother's face had crumpled up like a piece of paper. On it was written a love note to my father. Ever since they had come to this country, their life together was a constant war. "This is America, Papi, America!" she reminded him now. "You are not in a savage country any more!"

I was on my knees, weeping wildly, collecting all the little pieces of my speech, hoping that I could put it back together before the assembly tomorrow morning. But not even a sibyl could have made sense of all those scattered pieces of paper. All hope was lost. "He broke it, he broke it," I moaned as I picked up a handful of pieces.

Probably, if I had thought a moment about it, I would not have done what I did next. I would have realized my father had lost brothers and comrades to the dictator Trujillo. For the rest of his life, he would be haunted by blood in the streets and late night disappearances. Even after he had been in the states for years, he jumped if a black Volkswagen passed him on the street. He feared anyone in uniform: the meter maid giving out parking tickets, a museum guard approaching to tell him not to touch his favorite Goya at the Metropolitan.

I took a handful of the scraps I had gathered, stood up, and hurled them in his face. "Chapita!" I said in a low, ugly whisper. "You're just another Chapita!"

It took my father only a moment to register the hated nickname of our dictator, and he was after me. Down the halls we raced, but I was quicker than he and made it to my room just in time to lock the door as my father threw his weight against it. He called down curses on my head, ordered me on his authority as my father to open that door this very instant! He throttled that doorknob, but all to no avail. My mother's love of gadgets saved my hide that night. She had hired a locksmith to install good locks on all the bedroom doors after our house had been broken into while we were away the previous summer. In case burglars broke in again, and we were in the house, they'd have a second round of locks to contend with before they got to us.

"Eduardo," she tried to calm him down. "Don't you ruin my new locks."

He finally did calm down, his anger spent. I heard their footsteps retreating down the hall. I heard their door close, the clicking of their lock. Then, muffled voices, my mother's peaking in anger, in persuasion, my father's deep murmurs of explanation and of self-defense. At last, the house fell silent, before I heard, far off, the gun blasts and explosions, the serious, self-important voices of newscasters reporting their TV war.

A little while later, there was a quiet knock at my door, followed by a tentative attempt at the doorknob. "Cukita?" my mother whispered. "Open up, Cukita."

"Go away," I wailed, but we both knew I was glad she was there, and I needed only a moment's protest to save face before opening that door.

What we ended up doing that night was putting together a speech at the last moment. Two brief pages of stale compliments and the polite commonplaces on teachers, wrought by necessity without much invention by mother for daughter late into the night in the basement on the pad of paper and with the same pencil she had once used for her own inventions, for I was too upset to compose the speech myself. After it was drafted, she typed it up while I stood by, correcting her misnomers and mis-sayings.

She was so very proud of herself when I came home the next day with the success story of the assembly. The nuns had been flattered, the audience had stood up and given "our devoted teachers a standing ovation," what my mother had suggested they do at the end of my speech.

She clapped her hands together as I recreated the moment for her. "I stole that from your father's speech, remember? Remember how he put that in at the end?" She quoted him in Spanish, then translated for me into English.

That night, I watched him from the upstairs hall window where I'd retreated the minute I heard his car pull up in front of our house. Slowly, my father came up the driveway, a grim expression on his face as he grappled with a large, heavy cardboard box. At the front door, he set the package down carefully and patted all his pockets for his house keys—precisely why my mother had invented her ticking key chain. I heard the snapping open of the locks downstairs. Heard as he struggled to maneuver the box through the narrow doorway. Then, he called my name several times. But I would not answer him.

"My daughter, your father, he love you very much," he explained from the bottom of the stairs. "He just want to protect you." Finally, my mother came up and pleaded with me to go down and reconcile with him. "Your father did not mean to harm. You must pardon him. Always it is better to let bygones be forgotten, no?"

I guess she was right. Downstairs, I found him setting up a brand new electric typewriter on the kitchen table. It was even better than the one I'd been begging to get like my mother's. My father had outdone himself with all the extra features: a plastic carrying case with my initials, in decals, below the handle, a brace to lift the paper upright while I typed, an erase cartridge, an automatic margin tab, a plastic hood like a toaster cover to keep the dust away. Not even my mother, I think, could have invented such a machine!

But her inventing days were over just as mine were starting up with my schoolwide success. That's why I've always thought of that speech my mother wrote for me as her last invention rather than the suitcase rollers everyone else in the family remembers. It was as if she had passed on to me her pencil and pad and said, "Okay, Cukita, here's the buck. You give it a shot."

Geraldo No Last Name

Sandra Cisneros

SHE met him at a dance. Pretty too, and young. Said he worked in a restaurant, but she can't remember which one. Geraldo. That's all. Green pants and Saturday shirt. Geraldo. That's what he told her.

And how was she to know she'd be the last one to see him alive. An accident, don't you know. Hit and run. Marin, she goes to all those dances. Uptown. Logan. Embassy. Palmer. Aragon. Fontana. The manor. She likes to dance. She knows how to do cumbias and salsas and rancheras even. And he was just someone she danced with. Somebody she met that night. That's right.

That's the story. That's what she said again and again. Once to the hospital people and twice to the police. No address. No name. Nothing in his pockets. Ain't it a shame.

Only Marin can't explain why it mattered, the hours and hours, for somebody she didn't even know. The hospital emergency room. Nobody but an intern working all alone. And maybe if the surgeon would've come, maybe if he hadn't lost so much blood, if the surgeon had only come, they would know who to notify and where.

But what difference does it make? He wasn't anything to her. He wasn't her boyfriend or anything like that. Just another brazer who didn't speak English. Just another wetback. You know the kind. The ones who always look ashamed. And what was she doing out at 3:00 A.M. anyway? Marin who was sent home with her coat and some aspirin. How does she explain?

She met him at a dance. Geraldo in his shiny shirt and green pants. Geraldo going to a dance.

What does it matter?

They never saw the kitchenettes. They never knew about the two-room flats and sleeping rooms he rented, the weekly money orders sent home, the currency exchange. How could they?

His name was Geraldo. And his home is in another country. The ones he left behind are far away, will wonder, shrug, remember. Geraldo—he went north . . . we never heard from him again.

An Hour With Abuelo

Judith Ortiz Cofer

"JUST one hour, *una hora,* is all I'm asking of you, son." My grandfather is in a nursing home in Brooklyn, and my mother wants me to spend some time with him, since the doctors say that he doesn't have too long to go now. *I* don't have much time left of my summer vacation, and there's a stack of books next to my bed I've got to read if I'm going to get into the AP English class I want. I'm going stupid in some of my classes, and Mr. Williams, the principal at Central, said that if I passed some reading tests, he'd let me move up.

Besides, I hate the place, the old people's home, especially the way it smells like industrial-strength ammonia and other stuff I won't mention, since it turns my stomach. And really the abuelo always has a lot of relatives visiting him, so I've gotten out of going out there except at Christmas, when a whole vanload of grandchildren are herded over there to give him gifts and a hug. We all make it quick and spend the rest of the time in the recreation area, where they play checkers and stuff with some of the old people's games, and I catch up on back issues of *Modern Maturity.* I'm not picky, I'll read almost anything.

Anyway, after my mother nags me for about a week, I let her drive me to Golden Years. She drops me off in front. She wants me to go in alone and have a "good time" talking to Abuelo. I tell her to be back in one hour or I'll take the bus back to Paterson. She squeezes my hand and says, *"Gracias, hijo,"* in a choked-up voice like I'm doing her a big favor.

I get depressed the minute I walk into the place. They line up the old people in wheelchairs in the hallway as if they were about to be raced to the finish line by orderlies who don't even look at them when they push them here and there. I walk fast to room 10, Abuelo's "suite." He is sitting up in his bed writing with a pencil in one of those old-fashioned black hardback notebooks. It has the outline of the island of Puerto Rico on it. I slide into the hard vinyl chair by his bed. He sort of smiles and the lines on his face get deeper, but he doesn't say anything. Since I'm supposed to talk to him, I say, "What are you doing, Abuelo, writing the story of your life?"

It's supposed to be a joke, but he answers, "Sí, how did you know, Arturo?"

His name is Arturo too. I was named after him. I don't really know my grandfather. His children, including my mother, came to New York and New Jersey (where I was born) and he stayed on the Island until my grandmother died. Then he got sick, and since nobody could leave their jobs to go take care of him, they brought him to this nursing home in Brooklyn. I see him a couple of times a year, but he's always surrounded by his sons and daughters. My mother tells me that Don Arturo had once been a teacher back in Puerto Rico, but had lost his job after the war. Then he became a farmer. She's always saying in a sad voice, "Ay, bendito! What a waste of a fine mind." Then she usually shrugs her shoulders and says, "Así es la vida." That's the way life is. It sometimes makes me mad that the adults I know just accept whatever crap is thrown at them because "that's the way things are." Not for me. I go after what I want.

Anyway, Abuelo is looking at me like he was trying to see into my head, but he doesn't say anything. Since I like stories, I decide I may as well ask him if he'll read me what he wrote.

I look at my watch: I've already used up twenty minutes of the hour I promised my mother.

Abuelo starts talking in his slow way. He speaks what my mother calls book English. He taught himself from a dictionary, and his words sound stiff, like he's sounding them out in his head before he says them. With his children he speaks Spanish, and that funny book English with us grandchildren. I'm surprised that he's still so sharp, because his body is shrinking like a crumpled-up brown paper sack with some bones in it. But I can see from looking into his eyes that the light is still on in there.

"It is a short story, Arturo. The story of my life. It will not take very much time to read it."

"I have time, Abuelo." I'm a little embarrassed that he saw me looking at my watch.

"Yes, hijo. You have spoken the truth. La verdad. You have much time."

Abuelo reads: "'I loved words from the beginning of my life. In the *campo* where I was born one of seven sons, there were few books. My mother read them to us over and over: the Bible, the stories of Spanish conquistadors and of pirates that she had read as a child and brought with her from the city of Mayagüez;

that was before she married my father, a coffee bean farmer; and she taught us words from the newspaper that a boy on a horse brought every week to her. She taught each of us how to write on a slate with chalks that she ordered by mail every year. We used those chalks until they were so small that you lost them between your fingers.

"'I always wanted to be a writer and a teacher. With my heart and my soul I knew that I wanted to be around books all of my life. And so against the wishes of my father, who wanted all his sons to help him on the land, she sent me to high school in Mayagüez. For four years I boarded with a couple she knew. I paid my rent in labor, and I ate vegetables I grew myself. I wore my clothes until they were thin as parchment. But I graduated at the top of my class! My whole family came to see me that day. My mother brought me a beautiful *guayabera*, a white shirt made of the finest cotton and embroidered by her own hands. I was a happy young man.

"'In those days you could teach in a country school with a high school diploma. So I went back to my mountain village and got a job teaching all grades in a little classroom built by the parents of my students.

"'I had books sent to me by the government. I felt like a rich man although the pay was very small. I had books. All the books I wanted! I taught my students how to read poetry and plays, and how to write them. We made up songs and put on shows for the parents. It was a beautiful time for me.

"'Then the war came, and the American President said that all Puerto Rican men would be drafted. I wrote to our governor and explained that I was the only teacher in the mountain village. I told him that the children would go back to the fields and grow up ignorant if I could not teach them their letters. I said that I thought I was a better teacher than a soldier. The governor did not answer my letter. I went into the U.S. Army.

"'I told my sergeant that I could be a teacher in the army. I could teach all the farm boys their letters so that they could read the instructions on the ammunition boxes and not blow themselves up. The sergeant said I was too smart for my own good, and gave me a job cleaning latrines. He said to me there is reading material for you there, scholar. Read the writing on the walls. I spent the war mopping floors and cleaning toilets.

"'When I came back to the Island, things had changed. You had to have a college degree to teach school, even the lower grades. My parents were sick, two of my brothers had been killed in the war, the others had stayed in Nueva York. I was the only one left to help the old people. I became a farmer. I married a good woman who gave me many good children. I taught them all how to read and write before they started school.'"

Abuelo then puts the notebook down on his lap and closes his eyes.

"*Así es la vida* is the title of my book," he says in a whisper, almost to himself. Maybe he's forgotten that I'm there.

For a long time he doesn't say anything else. I think that he's sleeping, but then I see that he's watching me through half-closed lids, maybe waiting for my opinion of his writing. I'm trying to think of something nice to say. I liked it and all, but not the title. And I think that he could've been a teacher if he had wanted to bad enough. Nobody is going to stop me from doing what I want with my life. I'm not going to let la vida get in my way. I want to discuss this with him, but the words are not coming into my head in Spanish just yet. I'm about to ask him why he didn't keep fighting to make his dream come true, when an old lady in hot-pink running shoes sort of appears at the door.

She is wearing a pink jogging outfit too. The world's oldest marathoner, I say to myself. She calls out to my grandfather in a flirty voice, "Yoo-hoo, Arturo, remember what day this is? It's poetry-reading day in the rec room! You promised us you'd read your new one today."

I see my abuelo perking up almost immediately. He points to his wheelchair, which is hanging like a huge metal bat in the open closet. He makes it obvious that he wants me to get it. I put it together, and with Mrs. Pink Running Shoes's help, we get him in it. Then he says in a strong deep voice I hardly recognize, "Arturo, get that notebook from the table, please."

I hand him another map-of-the-Island notebook—this one is red. On it in big letters it says, *POEMAS DE ARTURO.*

I start to push him toward the rec room, but he shakes his finger at me.

"Arturo, look at your watch now. I believe your time is over." He gives me a wicked smile.

Then with her pushing the wheelchair—maybe a little too fast—they roll down the hall. He is already reading from his notebook, and she's making bird noises. I look at my watch and the hour *is* up, to the minute. I can't help but think that my abuelo has been timing *me.* It cracks me up. I walk slowly down the hall toward the exit sign. I want my mother to have to wait a little. I don't want her to think that I'm in a hurry or anything.

American History

Judith Ortiz Cofer

I ONCE read in a "Ripley's Believe It or Not" column that Paterson, New Jersey, is the place where the Straight and Narrow (streets) intersect. The Puerto Rican tenement known as *El Building* was one block up from Straight. It was, in fact, the corner of Straight and Market; not "at" the corner, but *the* corner. At almost any hour of the day, El Building was like a monstrous jukebox, blasting out *salsas* from open windows at the residents, mostly new immigrants just up from the island, tried to drown out whatever they were currently enduring with loud music. But the day President Kennedy was shot there was a profound silence in El Building; even the abusive tongues of viragoes, the cursing of the unemployed, and the screeching of small children had been somehow muted. President Kennedy was a saint to these people. In fact, soon his photograph would be hung alongside the Sacred Heart and over the spiritist altars that many women kept in their apartments. He would become part of the hierarchy of martyrs they prayed to for favors that only one who had died for a cause would understand.

On the day that President Kennedy was shot, my ninth grade class had been out in the fenced playground of Public School Number 13. We had been given "free" exercise time and had been ordered by our P.E. teacher, Mr. DePalma, to "keep moving." That meant that the girls should jump rope and the boys toss basketballs through a hoop at the far end of the yard. He in the meantime would "keep an eye" on us from just inside the building.

It was a cold gray day in Paterson. The kind that warns of early snow. I was miserable, since I had forgotten my gloves, and my knuckles were turning red and raw from the jump rope. I was also taking a lot of abuse from the black girls for not turning the rope hard and fast enough for them.

"Hey, Skinny Bones, pump it, girl. Ain't you got no energy today?" Gail, the biggest of the black girls had the other end of the rope, yelled, "Didn't you eat your rice and beans and pork chops for breakfast today?"

The other girls picked up the "pork chops" and made it into a refrain: "pork chop, pork chop, did you eat your pork chop?"

They entered the double ropes in pairs and exited without tripping or missing a beat. I felt a burning on my cheeks and then my glasses fogged up so that I could not manage to coordinate the jump rope with Gail. The chill was doing to me what it always did; entering my bones, making me cry, humiliating me. I hated the city, especially in winter. I hated Public School Number 13. I hated my skinny flat-chested body, and I envied the black girls who could jump rope so fast that their legs became a blur. They always seemed to be warm while I froze.

There was only one source of beauty and light for me that school year. The only thing I had anticipated at the start of the semester. That was seeing Eugene. In August, Eugene and his family had moved into the only house on the block that had a yard and trees. I could see his place from my window in El Building. In fact, if I sat on the fire escape I was literally suspended above Eugene's backyard. It was my favorite spot to read my library books in the summer. Until that August the house had been occupied by an old Jewish couple. Over the years I had become part of their family, without their knowing it, of course, I had a view of their kitchen and their backyard, and though I could not hear what they said, I knew when they were arguing, when one of them was sick, and many other things. I knew all this by watching them at mealtimes. I could see their kitchen table, the sink, and the stove. During good times, he sat at the table and read his newspapers while she fixed the meals. If they argued, he would leave and the old woman would sit and stare at nothing for a long time. When one of them was sick, the other would come and get things from the kitchen and carry them out on a tray. The old man had died in June. The last week of school I had not seen him at the table at all. Then one day I saw that there was a crowd in the kitchen. The old woman had finally emerged from the house on the arm of a stocky, middle-aged woman, whom I had seen there a few times before, maybe her daughter. Then a man had carried out suitcases. The house had stood empty for weeks. I had had to resist the temptation to climb down into the yard and water the flowers the old lady had taken such good care of.

By the time Eugene's family moved in, the yard was a tangled mass of weeds. The father had spent several days mowing, and when he finished, from where I sat, I didn't see the red, yellow, and purple clusters that meant flowers to me. I didn't see this family sit down at the kitchen table together. It was just the mother, a red-headed tall woman who wore a white uniform—a nurse's, I guessed it was; the father was gone before I got up in the morning and was never there at dinner time. I only saw him on weekends when they sometimes sat on lawn chairs under the oak tree, each hidden behind a section of the newspaper; and there was Eugene. He was tall and blond, and he wore glasses. I liked him right away because he sat at the kitchen table and read books for hours. That summer, before we had even spoken one word to each other, I kept him company on my fire escape.

Once school started I looked for him in all my classes, but P.S. 13 was a huge, overpopulated place and it took me days and many discreet questions to discover that Eugene was in honors classes for all his subjects; classes that were not open to me because English was not my first language, though I was a straight A student. After much maneuvering, I managed "to run into him" in the hallway where his locker was—on the other side of the building from mine—and in study hall at the library where he first seemed to notice me, but did not speak; and finally, on the way home after school one day when I decided to approach him directly, though my stomach was doing somersaults.

I was ready for rejection, snobbery, the worst. But when I came up to him, practically panting in my nervousness, and blurted out: "You're Eugene. Right?" he smiled, pushed his glasses up on his nose, and nodded. I saw then that he was blushing deeply. Eugene liked me, but he was shy. I did most of the talking that day. He nodded and smiled a lot. In the weeks that followed, we walked home together. He would linger at the corner of El Building for a few minutes then walk down to his two-story house. It was not until Eugene moved into that house that I noticed that El Building blocked most of the sun, and that the only spot that got a little sunlight during the day was the tiny square of earth the old woman had planted with flowers.

I did not tell Eugene that I could see inside his kitchen from my bedroom. I felt dishonest, but I liked my secret sharing of his evenings, especially now that I knew what he was reading since we chose our books together at the school library.

One day my mother came into my room as I was sitting on the window-sill staring out. In her abrupt way she said: "Elena, you are acting 'moony.'" *Enamorada* was what she really said, that is—like a girl stupidly infatuated. Since I had turned fourteen and started menstruating my mother had been more vigilant than ever. She acted as if I was going to go crazy or explode or something if she didn't watch me and nag me all the time about being a *señorita* now. She kept talking about virtue, morality, and other subjects that did not interest me in the least. My mother was unhappy in Paterson, but my father had a good job at the bluejeans factory in Passaic and soon, he kept assuring us, we would be moving to our own house there. Every Sunday we drove out to the suburbs of Paterson, Clifton, and Passaic, out to where people mowed grass on Sundays in the summer, and where children made snowmen in the winter from pure white snow, not like the gray slush of Paterson which seemed to fall from the sky in that hue. I had learned to listen to my parents' dreams, which were spoken in Spanish, as fairy tales, like the stories about life in the island paradise of Puerto Rico before I was born. I had been to the island once as a little girl, to grandmother's funeral, and all I remembered was wailing women in black, my mother becoming hysterical and being given a pill that made her sleep two days, and me feeling lost in a crowd of strangers all claiming to be my aunts, uncles, and cousins. I had actually been glad to return to the city. We had not been back there since then, though my parents talked constantly about buying a house on the beach someday, retiring on the island—that was a common topic among the residents of El Building. As for me, I was going to go to college and become a teacher.

But after meeting Eugene I began to think of the present more than of the future. What I wanted now was to enter that house I had watched for so many years. I wanted to see the other rooms where the old people had lived, and where the boy spent his time. Most of all, I wanted to sit at the kitchen table with Eugene like two adults, like the old man and his wife had done, maybe drink some coffee and talk about books. I had started reading *Gone with the Wind*. I was enthralled by it, with the daring and the passion of the beautiful girl living in a mansion, and with her devoted parents and the slaves who did everything for them. I didn't believe such a world had ever really existed, and I wanted to ask Eugene some questions since he and his parents, he had told me, had come up from Georgia, the same place where the novel was set. His father worked for a company that had transferred him to Paterson. His mother was very unhappy, Eugene said, in his beautiful voice that rose and fell over words in a strange, lilting way. The kids at school called him "the hick" and made fun of the way he talked. I knew I was his only friend so far, and I liked that, though I felt sad for him sometimes. "Skinny Bones" and the "Hick" was what they called us at school when we were seen together.

The day Mr. DePalma came out into the cold and asked us to line up in front of him was the day that President Kennedy was shot. Mr. DePalma, a short, muscular man with slicked-down black hair, was the science teacher, P.E. coach, and disciplinarian at P.S. 13. He was the teacher to whose homeroom you got assigned if you were a troublemaker, and the man called out to break up playground fights, and to escort violently angry teenagers to the office. And Mr. DePalma was the man who called your parents in for "a conference."

That day, he stood in front of two rows of mostly black and Puerto Rican kids, brittle from their efforts to "keep moving" on a November day that was turning bitter cold. Mr. DePalma, to our complete shock, was crying. Not just silent adult tears, but really sobbing. There was a few titters from the back of the line where I stood shivering.

"Listen," Mr. DePalma raised his arms over his head as if he were about to conduct an orchestra. His voice broke, and he covered his face with his hands. His barrel chest was heaving. Someone giggled behind me.

"Listen," he repeated, "something awful has happened." A strange gurgling came from his throat, and he turned around and spat on the cement behind him.

"Gross," someone said, and there was a lot of laughter.

"The President is dead, you idiots. I should have known that wouldn't mean anything to a bunch of losers like you kids. Go home." He was shrieking now. No one moved for a minute or two, but then a big girl let out a "Yeah!" and ran to get her books piled up with the others against the brick wall of the school building. The others followed in a mad scramble to get to their things before somebody caught on. It still an hour to the dismissal bell.

A little scared, I headed for El Building. There was an eerie feeling on the streets. I looked into Mario's drugstore, a favorite hangout for the high school crowd, but there were only a couple of old Jewish men at the soda-bar talking with the short order cook in tones that sounded almost angry, but they were keeping their voices low. Even the traffic on one of the busiest intersections in Paterson—Straight Street and Park Avenue—seemed to be moving slower. There were no horns blasting that day. At El Building, the usual little group of unemployed men were not hanging out on the front stoop making it difficult for women to enter the front door. No music spilled out from open doors in the hallway. When I walked into our apartment, I found my mother sitting in front of the grainy picture of the television set.

She looked up at me with a tear-streaked face and just said: *"Dios mio,"* turning back to the set as if it were pulling at her eyes. I went into my room.

Though I wanted to feel the right thing about President Kennedy's death, I could not fight the feeling of elation that stirred in my chest. Today was the day I was to visit Eugene in his house. He had asked me to come over after school to study for an American history test with him. We had also planned to walk to the public library together. I looked down into his yard. The oak tree was bare of leaves and the ground looked gray with ice. The light through the large kitchen window of his house told me that El Building blocked the sun to such an extent that they had to turn lights on in the middle of the day. I felt ashamed about it. But the white kitchen table with the lamp hanging just above it looked cozy and inviting. I would soon sit there, across from Eugene, and I would tell him about my perch just above his house. Maybe I should.

In the next thirty minutes I changed clothes, put on a little pink lipstick, and got my books together. Then I went in to tell my mother that I was going to a friend's house to study. I did not expect her reaction.

"You are going out *today?*" The way she said "today" sounded as if a storm warning had been issued. It was said in utter disbelief. Before I could answer, she came toward me and held my elbows as I clutched my books.

"*Hija,* the President has been killed. We must show respect. He was a great man. Come to church with me tonight."

She tried to embrace me, but my books were in the way. My first impulse was to comfort her, she seemed so distraught, but I had to meet Eugene in fifteen minutes.

"I have a test to study for, Mama. I will be home by eight."

"You are forgetting who you are, *Niña.* I have seen you staring down at that boy's house. You are heading for humiliation and pain." My mother said this in Spanish and in a resigned tone that surprised me, as if she had no intention of stopping me from "heading for humiliation and pain." I started for the door. She sat in front of the TV holding a white handkerchief to her face.

I walked out to the street and around the chainlink fence that separated El Building from Eugene's house. The yard was neatly edged around the little walk that led to the door. It always amazed me how Paterson, the inner core of the city, had no apparent logic to its architecture. Small, neat, single residences like this one could be found right next to huge, dilapidated apartment buildings like El Building. My guess was that the little houses had been there first, then the immigrants had come in droves, and the monstrosities had been raised for them—the Italians, the Irish, the Jews, and now us, the Puerto Ricans and the blacks. The door was painted a deep green: *verde*, the color of hope, I had heard my mother say it: *Verde-Esperanza*.

I knocked softly. A few suspenseful moments later the door opened just a crack. The red, swollen face of a woman appeared. She had a halo of red hair floating over a delicate ivory face—the face of a doll—with freckles on the nose. Her smudged eye make-up made her look unreal to me, like a mannequin seen through a warped store window.

"What do you want?" Her voice was tiny and sweet-sounding, like a little girl's, but her tone was not friendly.

"I'm Eugene's friend. He asked me over. To study." I thrust out my books, a silly gesture that embarrassed me almost immediately.

"You live there?" She pointed up to El Building, which looked particularly ugly, like a gray prison with its many dirty windows and rusty fire escapes. The woman had stepped halfway out and I could see that she wore a white nurse's uniform with St. Joseph's Hospital on the name tag.

"Yes. I do."

She looked intently at me for a couple of heartbeats, then said as if to herself, "I don't know how you people do it." Then directly to me: "Listen. Honey. Eugene doesn't want to study with you. He is a smart boy. Doesn't need help. You understand me. I am truly sorry if he told you you could come over. He cannot study with you. It's nothing personal. You understand? We won't be in this place much longer, no need for him to get close to people—it'll just make it harder for him later. Run back home now."

I couldn't move. I just stood there in shock at hearing these things said to me in such a honey-drenched voice. I had never heard an accent like hers, except for Eugene's softer version. It was as if she were singing me a little song.

"What's wrong? Didn't you hear what I said?" She seemed very angry, and I finally snapped out of my trance. I turned away from the green door, and heard her close it gently.

Our apartment was empty when I got home. My mother was in someone else's kitchen, seeking the solace she needed. Father would come in from his late shift at midnight. I would hear them talking softly in the kitchen for hours that night. They would not discuss their dreams for the future, or life in Puerto Rico, as they often did; that night they would talk sadly about the young widow and her two children, as if they were family. For the next few days, we would observe *luto* in our apartment; that is, we would practice restraint and silence—no loud music or laughter. Some of the women of El Building would wear black for weeks.

That night, I lay in my bed trying to feel the right thing for our dead President. But the tears that came up from a deep source inside me were strictly for me. When my mother came to the door, I pretended to be sleeping. Sometime during the night, I saw from my bed the streetlight come on. It had a pink halo around it. I went to my window and pressed my face to the cool glass. Looking up at the light I could see the white snow falling like a lace veil over its face. I did not look down to see it turning gray as it touched the ground below.

Distillation

Hugo Martínez-Serros

HE went on Saturdays because it was the best day. He did it for years and we, his sons, were his helpers. And yet one day alone remains, that single distant Saturday—a day so different from the rest that I cannot forget it:

Friday night I was in bed by nine. It would take us about an hour to get there, and we had to leave by eight the following morning to arrive just before the first tall trucks. All day the trucks would come and go, all day until five in the afternoon. My father wanted to get there before anyone else. He wanted to look it all over and then swoop down on the best places. There the spoils would go to the quickest hands, and we would work in swift thrusts, following his example, obeying the gestures and words he used to direct us.

That Saturday morning my father waited impatiently for us, his piercing whistles shrilling his annoyance at our delay. Anxious for us, my mother pushed us through the door as she grazed us with her lips. My father was flicking at his fingers with a rag and turned sharply to glower at us. I saw fresh grease on the hubs of the big iron wheels that supported the weight of his massive wagon, its great wooden bed and sides fixed on heavy steel axletrees. He spoke harshly to us, for we had kept him waiting and he was angry: "What took you so long? ¡Vámonos!"

He had already lowered the wagon's sides. Now, grasping us at the armpits, he picked us up and set us in beside the burlap sacks and a bag of food, starting with me, the youngest, and following the order of our ages—five, six and a half, eight, and eleven. He handed us a gallon jug of water and then pulled the guayín through the door in the backyard fence, easing it out into the alley by the very long shaft that was its handle, like some vaguely familiar giant gently drawing a ship by its prow.

Yawning in the warmth of May, I leaned back, like my brothers, in anticipation of the joys of a crossing that would reach almost the full length of the longest line that could be drawn in the world as I knew it. That world, dense and more durable than a name, extended just beyond South Chicago. The day, a vast blue balloon stretched to its limits by a great flood of light, contained us and invited our blinking eyes to examine all that it enveloped.

The fastest route led us down alleys, away from pedestrians, cars, trucks and wide horse-drawn wagons that plied the streets. The alleys, always familiar, seemed somehow new in the morning light that gleamed on piles of garbage and everywhere flashed slivers of rainbows in beads of moisture. Garbage men used shovels to clear away these piles. What garbage cans there were stood sheltered against walls and fences or lay fallen in heaps of refuse. Through the unpaved alleys we went, over black earth hard packed and inlaid with myriad fragments of glass that sparkled in the morning radiance. Ahead of us rats scattered, fleeing the noise and bulk that moved toward them. Stray dogs, poking their noses into piles, did not retreat at our approach. Sunlight and shadows mottled my vision as the wagon rolled past trees, poles, fences, garages, sheds. My father moved in and out of the light, in and out of the shadows. On clotheslines, threadbare garments waved and swelled. Without slowing down, my father navigated around potholes, and these sudden maneuvers shook loose squeals and laughter as our bodies swayed.

At 86th Street he had to leave the alleys to continue south. There the steel mills and train yards suddenly closed in on us. We rattled over the railroad crossing at Burley Avenue, a busy, noisy pass, and this made me stiffen and press my palms against my ears. For one block Burley Avenue was a corridor—the only one for some distance around—that allowed movement north and south. At 89th Street my father followed a southwesterly course, going faster and faster, farther and farther from the steel mills, moving beyond the commercial area into a zone where the houses looked more and more expensive and the lawns grew thicker and greener. Already there were many flowers here, but no noise and few children, and there were no alleys. As my father rushed through these neighborhoods, we fell silent. I was baffled by the absence of garbage, and my eyes searched for an explanation that was to remain hidden from me for years.

At the end of a street that advanced between rows of brick bungalows stood the tunnel. We entered it and I tensed, at once exhilarated and alarmed by the wagon's din, frightened by the sudden darkness yet braving it because my father was there. A long time passed before we reached midpoint, where I feared everything would cave in on us. Then slowly my father's silhouette, pillarlike, filled the space ahead of me, growing larger and larger as we approached the light. Beyond the tunnel there were no houses, and we emerged into the radiance of 95th Street and Torrence Avenue.

There, stopping for the traffic that raced along 95th Street, my father quickly harnessed himself to the wagon with the double rope that was coiled around its prowlike handle. He was safe in this rude harness, for he could loosen it instantly and drop back alongside the great vehicle to brake it if the need arose. Now he pulled his wagon into Torrence Avenue, and his legs pumped, hard at first, and then they let up and soon he was running. Torrence Avenue, broad and well paved, shone like still water, and he ran smoothly, with long strides, at about three quarters of his top speed. We were smiling now, and we saw the smile on his face when he looked back over his shoulder. Breathing easily, he ran before us, and I watched his effortless movement forward. I felt a sudden keen desire to be just like him and for an instant found it difficult to breathe. To our right was a green expanse—trees, wildflowers, grasses, and a bountiful variety of weeds—like a green sea extending to the horizon. Torrence Avenue now curved gently to the left for a half block and farther ahead gradually straightened along a stretch of several blocks, flanked on the left by a high fence and a long dense row of poplars. As my father navigated out of the curve we urged him on.

"Faster, Pa, faster! ¡Más rápido!"

"Come on, Pa, you c'n go faster'n that!"

"Pa, as fast as you c'n go, Pa, as fast as you c'n go!"

"Like a car, Pa, like a car!"

The prow shot forward, chasing my father as he reached top speed, and the craft darted into the straight lane that would take us to 103rd Street. My heart unleashed and racing, I looked up into the row of trees at the shoreline, saw swift islets of blue sky coursing brightly through the green current of foliage. Along the shoreline my father's pace gradually slowed until he seemed to be moving at half speed. Whenever he glanced backward, we saw sweat trickling down his forehead and following the line of his eyebrows to join the streamlets running from his temples. Beads of perspiration swelled at his hairline and slid down his neck into the blue denim shirt, which deepened to a dolphin color. Far beyond the fence, their smoking stacks thrust into the sky, the steel mills took on the appearance of enormous, dark, steam-driven vessels.

At 103rd Street my father veered due west. Ahead of us, at a distance of several blocks, loomed the 103rd Street Bridge. All his pacing had led to this, was a limbering up for this assent. Many yards before the street rose, my father began to increase his speed with every stride. He did it gradually, never slackening, for the wagon was heavy and accelerated slowly. I placed the gallon jug of water between my legs and tightened them around it as he reached full speed just before storming the incline. He started up unfalteringly, tenaciously, with short, rapid steps and his body bent forward, his natural reaction to the exaggerated resistance suddenly offered by the wagon. From a point high in the sky the pavement poured down on us. Immediately my father was drenched in sweat. His face, in profile now on the left, now on the right, became twisted with exertion while his broad back grew to twice its size under the strain. We held our breath, maintained a fragile silence, and did not move, our bodies taut from participation in his struggle. All the way up we lost speed by degrees. His breathing grew heavy, labored. His legs slowed, seeking now to recover with more powerful thrusts what they had lost with a diminished number of strokes. His jaw tightened, his head fell, sometimes he closed his eyes, and we could see his tortured face as his arms swung desperately at some invisible opponent, and still he went up, up, up.

When the pavement leveled off, he yielded for a moment, broke into a smile, and then, summoning reserves from the labyrinth of his will, lunged forward furiously, as if galvanized by his victory, and reached full speed at the moment the wagon began to descend. Miraculously, he freed himself from the harness, turned the shaft back into the wagon, and jumped on. Winking at us, he fell to his knees and leaned hard on the shaft. He was happy, wildly happy, and saw that we were too, and he laughed without restraint. "Miren, vean, look around you!" he shouted to us.

We were at the summit and the world fell away from us far into the horizon. To the east, steel mills, granaries, railroad yards, a profusion of industrial plants; to the north and south, prairies, trees, some houses; to the west, main arteries, more plants, the great smoking heaps of the city dump, and, farther still, houses and a green sweep of trees that extended as far as the eye saw. Years have changed this area in many ways, but that landscape, like a photo negative, glows in memory's light.

We had churned up the mountainous wave of the bridge, and now, as we coasted down ever faster, we screeched and I could feel my body pucker. Our excitement was different now. It came of expectancy, of the certain knowledge that we would soon be sailing. We were safe with our incomparable pilot, but we howled with nervous delight as we picked up speed. Down, down, straight down we fell, and then the guayín righted itself and my stomach shot forward, threatening for a fraction of a second to move beyond its body.

When the wagon finally came to a stop, my father got down. Again he harnessed himself to it and pulled us onward. He moved with haste but did not run. Looking into the immense blue dome above us, we knew our journey would soon end and we began to shift uneasily, anticipating our arrival. With cupped hands we covered our faces and grew silent while the wheels beneath us seemed to clack-clack louder and louder each time they passed over the pavement lines. At the divided highway my father turned south. We would be there in minutes.

The wagon stopped. We dropped our hands, exposing our faces, and climbed down. The full stink of decomposing garbage, fused to that of slow-burning trash, struck us. Before us was the city dump—a great raw sore on the landscape, a leprous tract oozing flames and smoldering, hellish grounds columned in smoke and grown tumid across years. Fragments of glass, metal, wood, lay everywhere, some of them menacingly jagged where they had not been driven into the earth by the wheels of the ponderous trucks.

My father had learned that the dump yielded more and better on Saturdays. Truckloads of spoiled produce were dumped that day, truckloads from warehouses, markets, stores, truckloads of stale or damaged food. We would spend the entire day here, gathering, searching, sifting, digging, following the trucks' shifting centers of activity.

Along a network of roads that crisscrossed the dumping grounds, trucks lumbered to and fro, grinding forward over ruts, jerking backward, all of them rocking from side to side. My father took some burlap sacks, scanned the area, and pointed to the site where we would work. He went toward it quickly, followed by my oldest brothers. Lázaro and I stationed the wagon beyond reach of the clumsy vehicles that were already dumping and then made our way to the site. We started to work on a huge pile of deteriorating fruit, picking only what a paring knife would later make edible.

After several trips to the wagon, my father and brothers moved on to other piles. My job was to stay and guard the wagon, neatly arranging all that went into it. When I remembered, I took the jug of water and buried it in the earth to keep it cool. Eager for their company, I waited for my brothers to return with their newest finds.

From where I stood guard, I could see my father and brothers hurrying toward a truck that had just arrived. It was rumbling toward a dump area just beyond me. The men on that high, wobbly truck were pointing, nodding, waving—gestures signaling my father and brothers to follow because they carried a rich load. Directed by a man who advanced slowly and seemed to walk on his knees, the truck waded into a heap of garbage, dumped its cargo to the whir of a hydraulic mechanism, and was pulling out as my father and brothers drew close enough to express their gratitude with a slight movement of their heads.

Now my father waved to me. It was a call to join them before others arrived. As I started toward them, my brother Lázaro foundered on a spongy mass, fell through it, and disappeared. I stopped in my tracks, stunned. "Buried," I whispered, "he's buried!" My father saw him fall, bolted to his side, and thundered a command, "Alzate, Lázaro, get up, get up!" and in seconds he had raised him. Unsteady on his feet, Lázaro shook himself off like a wet dog and then brushed away scabs of rotting stuff that clung to him. Suddenly the stench of decay, the idea of grabbing something that might crumble into muck, the thought of losing my footing in all that garbage, filled me with terror. On tentative feet I went forward cautiously, expecting the ground to give way beneath me. My steps were becoming steady when one of them set off a long, frenzied squeak. A rat sprang from under my foot and retreated grudgingly, black eyes unblinking, sharp teeth flashing beneath bristly whiskers, long tail stiffly trailing its fat body. I did not move until my father's shrill whistle roused me; then he called me in an angry voice and I moved on.

Working in silence, we gathered what we wanted from that mound. Now and again the sun's oppressive heat was dimmed by clouds that seemed to come from nowhere, bringing us relief.

By noon the sky was overcast. We pulled the wagon away from the dumping area and sat on the ground to eat what we had brought from home. By then the stench no longer bothered us. My father handed us bean and potato tacos that were still warm.

Hunger made them exquisite, and I sat there chewing slowly, deliberately, making them last, too happy to say anything. We shared the jug of water, bits of damp earth clinging to our hands after we set it down.

Before us was the coming and going of trucks, the movement of men, rats scurrying everywhere, some dogs, and just beyond us, under a tentlike tarp, a big gas-powered pump that was used to drain water from that whole area, which flooded easily in a heavy rain. Behind us was a tiny shack, crudely assembled with cardboard, wood, and sheet metal, home of the dump's only dweller, Uñas. He was nowhere in sight, but my mind saw him—a monstrous dung beetle rolling balls endlessly, determination on his pockmarked face, jaws in constant motion and his hands thrashing nervously, searching the grounds with a frenzy unleashed by the appearance of intruders.

By 12:30 the sky's blue was completely eclipsed. Above us an ugly gray was pressing down the sky, flattening it by degrees. My father stood up and looked hard at the sky as he spun on his heel. The temperature dropped abruptly and a strong wind rose, blowing paper, cans, boxes, and other objects across the grounds in all directions. He issued orders rapidly: "¡Pronto! Block the wheels and cover the wagon with the lona! Tie it down!" Then he took a sack and hurried off to a heap he had been eyeing while we ate.

We leaped forward, the two youngest scurrying in search of something to anchor the wheels with, while the two eldest raised the wagon's sides and unfolded the tarp my father had designed for such an emergency. The wheels blocked, we turned to help our brothers. We had seen our father tie down the tarp many times. We pulled it taut over the wagon and carefully drew the ends down and under, tying securely the lengths of rope that hung from its edges.

Huddled around the wagon, we watched the day grow darker. Big black clouds, their outlines clearly visible, scudded across the sky. It was cold and we shivered in our shirt sleeves. Now the wind blew with such force that it lifted things and flung them into spasmodic flight. We moved in together and bent down to shield and anchor ourselves. Frightened, we held our silence and pressed in closer until one of us, pointing, gasped. "Look! No one's out there! No one! Jus' look! We're all alone!"

A bolt of lightening ripped the sky and a horrendous explosion followed. Terror gripped us and we began to wail. The clouds dumped their load of huge, cold drops. And suddenly my father appeared in the distance. He looked tiny as he ran, flailing his arms, unable to shout over the sound of wind and water. He was waving us into the shack and we obeyed at once. Inside, cowed by the roar outside and pressing together, we trembled as we waited for him. He had almost reached us when the wind sheared off the roof. Part of one side was blown away as the first small pebbles of ice began to fall. He was shouting as he ran, "Salgan, come out, come out!"

We tumbled out, arms extended as we groped toward him, clutched his legs when he reached us and pulled us away seconds before the wind leveled what remained of the shack. A knot of arms and legs, we stumbled to the wagon. There was no shelter for hundreds of yards around and we could not see more than several yards in front of us. The rain slashed down, diminished, and hail fell with increasing density as the size of the spheres grew. Now we cried out with pain as white marbles struck us. My father's head pitched furiously and he bellowed with authority, "¡Cállense! Be still! Don't move from here! I'll be right back, ahorita vuelvo!"

In seconds he was back, dragging behind him the huge tarp he had torn from the pump, moving unflinchingly under the cold jawbreakers that were pummeling us. With a powerful jerk he pulled it up his back and over his head, held out his arms like wings, and we instinctively darted under. The growing force of the hailstorm crashed down on him. Thrashing desperately under the tarp, we found his legs and clung to them. I crawled between them. We could not stop bawling.

Once more he roared over the din, "There's nothing to fear! ¡Nada! You're safe with me, you know that, ya lo saben!" And then little by little he lowered his voice until he seemed to be whispering, "I would never let anything harm you, nunca, nunca. Ya, cállense, cállense ya. Cálmense, be still, you're safe, seguros, you're with me, with Papá. It's going to end now, very soon, very soon, it'll end, you'll see, ya verán, ya verán. Be still, be still, you're with me, with me. Ya, ya, cállense. . . ."

Bent forward, he held fast, undaunted, fixed to the ground, and we tried to cast off our terror. Huddled under the wings of that spreading giant, we saw the storm release its savagery, hurl spheres of ice like missiles shot from slings. They came straight down, so dense that we could see only a few feet beyond us. Gradually the storm abated, and we watched the spheres bounce

with great elasticity from hard surfaces, carom when they col-
lided, spring from the wagon's tarp like golf balls dropped on
blacktopped streets. When it stopped hailing, the ground lay hidden under a vast white beaded quilt. At a distance from us and
down, the highway was a string of stationary vehicles with their
lights on. Repeatedly, bright bolts of lightning tore the sky from
zenith to horizon and set off detonations that seemed to come
from deep in the earth. At last the rain let up. My father straightened himself, rose to his full height, and we emerged from the
tarp as it slid from us with a movement of his head and eyes,
and as he calmly flexed his arms, the four of us struggled to
cover the damaged pump with his great canvas mantle.

His unexpected "¡Vámonos!" filled us with joy and we prepared
to leave. Hail and water were cleared from the wagon's cover. My
brothers and I dug through the ice to free the wheels, and when
my father took up the handle and pulled, we pushed from behind with all our might, slipping, falling, rising, moving the
wagon forward by inches, slowly gaining a little speed, and finally holding at a steady walk to keep from losing control. Where
the road met the highway, we waded through more than a foot of
water and threw our shoulders into the wagon to shove it over
the last bump. Long columns of stalled cars lined the highway as
drivers examined dents and shattered or broken windows and
windshields. We went home in a dense silence, my father steer-
ing and pulling in front, we propelling from behind.

Entering the yard from the alley, we unloaded the wagon without delay. While my father worked his wagon into the coal shed
and locked the door, my brothers and I carried the sacks up to
our second-floor flat. It was almost four when we finished emp-
tying the sacks on newspapers spread on the kitchen floor.
There we began to pare while my mother, scrubbing carefully,
washed in the sink. We chattered furiously, my brothers and I,
safe now from the danger outside.

Lázaro brought the knife down on the orange, the orange
slipped from his hand, and the blade cut the tip of his thumb.
He held his thumb in his fist and I got up to bring him gauze
and tape from the bathroom. I knew my father would let me in
even if he had already started to bathe.

Some object fallen between the bathroom door and its frame
had kept it ajar, but he did not hear me approach. I froze. He
was standing naked beside a heap of clothes, running his hands

over his arms and shoulders, his fingertips pausing to examine more closely. His back and arms were a mass of ugly welts, livid flesh that had been flailed again and again until the veins beneath the skin had broken. His arms dropped to his sides and I thought I saw him shudder. Suddenly he seemed to grow, to swell, to fill the bathroom with his great mass. Then he threw his head back, shaking his black mane, smiled, stepped into the bathtub, and immersed himself in the water. Without knowing why, I waited a moment before timidly entering—even as I have paused all these years, and pause still, in full knowledge now, before entering that distant Saturday.

Mr. Mendelsohn

Nicholasa Mohr

"PSST . . . PSST, Mr. Mendelsohn, wake up. Come on now!"
Mrs. Suárez said in a low quiet voice. Mr. Mendelsohn had fallen
asleep again, on the large armchair in the living room. He
grasped the brown shiny wooden cane and leaned forward, his
chin on his chest. The small black skullcap that was usually
placed neatly on the back of his head had tilted to one side, covering his right ear. "Come on now. It's late, and time to go home."
She tapped him on the shoulder and waited for him to wake up.
Slowly, he lifted his head, opened his eyes, and blinked.

"What time is it?" he asked.

"It's almost midnight. Caramba! I didn't even know you was
still here. When I came to shut off the lights, I saw you was
sleeping."

"Oh . . . I'm sorry. Okay, I'm leaving." With short, slow steps
he followed Mrs. Suárez over to the front door.

"Go on now," she said, opening the door. "We'll see you
tomorrow."

He walked out into the hallway, stepped about three feet to
the left, and stood before the door of his apartment. Mrs. Suárez
waited, holding her door ajar while he carefully searched for the
right key to each lock. He had to open seven locks in all.

A small fluffy dog standing next to Mrs. Suárez began to
whine and bark.

"Shh-sh, Sporty! Stop it!" she said. "You had your walk. Shh."

"Okay," said Mr. Mendelsohn, finally opening his door. "Good
night." Mrs. Suárez smiled and nodded.

"Good night," she whispered as they both shut their doors
simultaneously.

Mr. Mendelsohn knocked on the door and waited; then tried the
doorknob. Turning and pushing, he realized the door was
locked, and knocked again, this time more forcefully. He heard
Sporty barking and footsteps coming toward the door.

"Who's there?" a child's voice asked.

"It's me—Mr. Mendelsohn! Open up, Yvonne." The door
opened, and a young girl, age nine, smiled at him.

"Mami! It's el Señor Mr. Mendelsohn again."

"Tell him to come on in, muchacha!" Mrs. Suárez answered.

"My mother says come on in."

He followed Yvonne and the dog, who leaped up, barking and wagging his tail. Mr. Mendelsohn stood at the kitchen entrance and greeted everyone.

"Good morning to you all!" He had just shaved and trimmed his large black mustache. As he smiled broadly, one could see that most of his teeth were missing. His large bald head was partially covered by his small black skullcap. Thick dark gray hair grew in abundance at the lower back of his head, coming around the front above his ears into short sideburns. He wore a clean white shirt, frayed at the cuffs. His worn-out pinstripe trousers were held up by a pair of dark suspenders. Mr. Mendelsohn leaned on his brown shiny cane and carried a small brown paper bag.

"Mr. Mendelsohn, come into the kitchen," said Mrs. Suárez, "and have some coffee with us." She stood by the stove. A boy of eleven, a young man of about seventeen, and a young pregnant woman were seated at the table.

"Sit here," said the boy, vacating a chair. "I'm finished eating." He stood by the entrance with his sister Yvonne, and they both looked at Mr. Mendelsohn and his paper bag with interest.

"Thank you, Georgie," Mr. Mendelsohn said. He sat down and placed the bag on his lap.

The smell of freshly perked coffee and boiled milk permeated the kitchen.

Winking at everyone, the young man asked, "Hey, what you got in that bag you holding on to, huh, Mr. Mendelsohn?" They all looked at each other and at the old man, amused. "Something special, I bet!"

"Well," the old man replied, "I thought your mama would be so kind as to permit me to make myself a little breakfast here today . . . so." He opened the bag and began to take out its contents. "I got two slices of rye bread, two tea bags. I brought one extra, just in case anybody would care to join me for tea. And a jar of herring in sour cream."

"Sounds delicious!" said the young man, sticking out his tongue and making a face. Yvonne and Georgie burst out laughing.

"Shh . . . sh." Mrs. Suárez shook her head and looked at her children disapprovingly. "Never mind, Julio!" she said to the young man. Turning to Mr. Mendelsohn, she said, "You got the same like you brought last Saturday, eh? You can eat with us anytime. How about some fresh coffee? I just made it. Yes?" Mr. Mendelsohn looked at her, shrugging his shoulders. "Come on, have some," she coaxed.

"Okay," he replied. "If it's not too much bother."

"No bother," she said, setting out a place for the old man. "You gonna have some nice fresh bread with a little butter—it will go good with your herring." Mrs. Suárez cut a generous slice of freshly baked bread with a golden crust and buttered it. "Go on, eat. There's a plate and everything for your food. Go on, eat . . ."

"Would anyone care for some?" Mr. Mendelsohn asked. "Perhaps a tea bag for a cup of tea?"

"No . . . no thank you, Mr. Mendelsohn," Mrs. Suárez answered. "Everybody here already ate. You go ahead and eat. You look too skinny; you better eat. Go on, eat your bread."

The old man began to eat vigorously.

"Can I ask you a question?" Julio asked the old man. "Man, I don't get you. You got a whole apartment next door all to yourself—six rooms! And you gotta come here to eat in this crowded kitchen. Why?"

"First of all, today is Saturday, and I thought I could bring in my food and your mama could turn on the stove for me. You know, in my religion you can't light a fire on Saturday."

"You come here anytime. I turn on the stove for you, don't worry," Mrs. Suárez said.

"Man, what about other days? We been living here for about six months, right?" Julio persisted. "And you do more cooking here than in your own place."

"It doesn't pay to turn on the gas for such a little bit of cooking. So I told the gas company to turn it off . . . for good! I got no more gas now, only an electric hot plate," the old man said.

Julio shook his head and sighed. "I don't know—"

"Julio, chico!" snapped Mrs. Suárez, interrupting him, "Basta—it doesn't bother nobody." She looked severely at her son and shook her head. "You gotta go with your sister to the clinic today, so you better get ready now. You too, Marta."

"Okay, Mama," she answered, "but I wanted to see if I got mail from Ralphy today."

"You don't got time. I'll save you the mail, you read it when you get back. You and Julio better get ready. Go on." Reluctantly, Marta stood up and yawned, stretching and arching her back.

"Marta," Mr. Mendelsohn said, "you taking care? . . . You know, this is a very delicate time for you."

"I am, Mr. Mendelsohn. Thank you."

"I raised six sisters," the old man said. "I ought to know. Six . . . and married them off to fine husbands. Believe me, I've done my share in life." Yvonne and Georgie giggled and poked each other.

"He's gonna make one of his speeches," they whispered.

" . . . I never had children. No time to get married. My father died when I was eleven. I went to work supporting my mother and six younger sisters. I took care of them, and today they are all married, with families. They always call and want me to visit them. I'm too busy and I have no time . . ."

"Too busy eating in our kitchen," whispered Julio. Marta, Georgie, and Yvonne tried not to laugh out loud. Mrs. Suárez reached over and with a wooden ladle managed a light but firm blow on Julio's head.

". . . Only on the holidays, I make some time to see them. But otherwise, I cannot be bothered with all that visiting." Mr. Mendelsohn stopped speaking and began to eat again.

"Go on, Marta and Julio, you will be late for the clinic," Mrs. Suárez said. "And you two? What are you doing there smiling like two monkeys? Go find something to do!"

Quickly, Georgie and Yvonne ran down the hallway, and Julio and Marta left the kitchen.

Mrs. Suárez sat down beside the old man.

"Another piece of bread?" she asked.

"No, thank you very much . . . I'm full. But it was delicious."

"You too skinny—you don't eat right, I bet." Mrs. Suárez shook her head. "Come tomorrow and have Sunday supper with us."

"I really couldn't."

"Sure, you could. I always make a big supper and there is plenty. All right? Mr. Suárez and I will be happy to have you."

"Are you sure it will be no bother?"

"What are you talking for the bother all the time? One more person is no bother. You come tomorrow. Yes?"

The old man smiled broadly and nodded. This was the first time he had been invited to Sunday supper with the family.

Mrs. Suárez stood and began clearing away the dishes. "Okay, you go inside, listen to the radio or talk to the kids—or something. I got work to do."

Mr. Mendelsohn closed his jar of herring and put it back into the bag. "Can I leave this here till I go?"

"Leave it. I put it in the refrigerator for you."

Leaning on his cane, Mr. Mendelsohn stood up and walked out of the kitchen and down the long hallway into the living room. It was empty. He went over to a large armchair by the window. The sun shone through the window, covering the entire armchair and Mr. Mendelsohn. A canary cage was also by the window, and two tiny yellow birds chirped and hopped back and forth energetically. Mr. Mendelsohn felt drowsy; he shut his eyes. So many aches and pains, he thought. It was hard to sleep at night, but here, well . . . The birds began to chirp in unison and the old man opened one eye, glancing at them, and smiled. Then he shut his eyes once more and fell fast asleep.

When Mr. Mendelsohn opened his eyes, Georgie and Yvonne were in the living room. Yvonne held a deck of playing cards and Georgie read a comic book. She looked at the old man and, holding up the deck of cards, asked, "Do you wonna play a game of war? Huh, Mr. Mendelsohn?"

"I don't know how to play that," he answered.

"It's real easy. I'll show you. Come on . . . please!"

"Well," he shrugged, "sure, why not? Maybe I'll learn something."

Yvonne took a small maple end table and a wooden chair, and set them next to Mr. Mendelsohn. "Now," she began, "I'll shuffle the cards and you cut, and then I throw down a card and you throw down a card and the one with the highest card wins. Okay? And then, the one with the most cards of all wins the game. Okay?"

"That's all?" he asked.

"That's all. Ready?" she asked, and sat down. They began to play cards.

"You know, my sister Jennie used to be a great card player," said Mr. Mendelsohn.

"Does she still play?" asked Yvonne.

"Oh . . ." Mr. Mendelsohn laughed. "I don't know anymore. She's already married and has kids. She was the youngest in my family—like you."

"Did she go to P.S. Thirty-nine? On Longwood Avenue?"

"I'm sure she did. All my sisters went to school around here."

"Wow! You must be living here a long time, Mr. Mendelsohn."

"Forty-five years!" said the old man.

"Wowee!" Yvonne whistled. "Georgie, did you hear? Mr. Mendelsohn been living here for forty-five whole years!"

Georgie put down his comic book and looked up.

"Really?" he asked, impressed.

"Yes, forty-five years this summer we moved here. But in those days things were different, not like today. No sir! The

Bronx has changed. Then, it was the country. That's right! Why, look out the window. You see the elevated trains on Westchester Avenue? Well, there were no trains then. That was once a dirt road. They used to bring cows through there."

"Oh, man!" Georgie and Yvonne both gasped.

"Sure. These buildings were among the first apartment houses to go up. Four stories high, and that used to be a big accomplishment in them days. All that was here was mostly little houses, like you still see here and there. Small farms, woodlands . . . like that."

"Did you see any Indians?" asked Georgie.

"What do you mean, Indians?" laughed the old man. "I'm not that old, and this here was not the Wild West." Mr. Mendelsohn saw that the children were disappointed. He added quickly, "But we did have carriages with horses. No cars and lots of horses."

"That's what Mami says they have in Puerto Rico—not like here in El Bronx," said Yvonne.

"Yeah," Georgie agreed. "Papi says he rode a horse when he was a little kid in Puerto Rico. They had goats and pigs and all them things. Man, was he lucky."

"Lucky?" Mr. Mendelsohn shook his head. "You—you are the lucky one today! You got school and a good home and clothes. You don't have to go out to work and support a family like your papa and I had to do, and miss an education. You can learn and be somebody someday."

"Someday," said Yvonne, "we are gonna get a house with a yard and all. Mami says that when Ralphy gets discharged from the army, he'll get a loan from the government and we can pay to buy a house. You know, instead of rent."

Mrs. Suárez walked into the living room with her coat on, carrying a shopping bag.

"Yvonne, take the dog out for a walk, and Georgie, come on! We have to go shopping. Get your jacket."

Mr. Mendelsohn started to rise. "No," she said, "stay . . . sit down. It's okay. You can stay and rest if you want."

"All right, Mrs. Suárez," Mr. Mendelsohn said.

"Now don't forget tomorrow for Sunday supper, and take a nap if you like."

Mr. Mendelsohn heard the front door slam shut, and the apartment was silent. The warmth of the bright sun made him drowsy once more. It was so nice here, he thought, a house full of people and kids—like it used to be. He recalled his sisters and his parents . . . the holidays . . . the arguments . . . the laughing. It was so empty next door. He would have to look for a smaller apartment, near Jennie, someday. But not now. Now, it was just nice to sleep and rest right here. He heard the tiny birds chirping and quietly drifted into a deep sleep.

Mr. Mendelsohn rang the bell, then opened the door. He could smell the familiar cooking odors of Sunday supper. For two years he had spent every Sunday at his neighbors'. Sporty greeted him, jumping affectionately and barking.

"Sh—sh . . . down. Good boy," he said, and walked along the hallway toward the kitchen. The room was crowded with people and the stove was loaded with large pots of food, steaming and puffing. Mrs. Suárez was busy basting a large roast. Looking up, she saw Mr. Mendelsohn.

"Come in," she said, "and sit down." Motioning to Julio, who was seated, she continued, "Julio, you are finished, get up and give Mr. Mendelsohn a seat." Julio stood up.

"Here's the sponge cake," Mr. Mendelsohn said, and handed the cake box he carried to Julio, who put it in the refrigerator.

"That's nice, thank you," said Mrs. Suárez, and placed a cup of freshly made coffee before the old man.

"Would anyone like some coffee?" Mr. Mendelsohn asked. Yvonne and Georgie giggled, looked at one another, and shook their heads.

"You always say that!" said Yvonne.

"One of these days," said Ralphy, "I'm gonna say, 'Yes, give me your coffee,' and you won't have none to drink." The children laughed loudly.

"Don't tease him," Mrs. Suárez said, half smiling. "Let him have his coffee."

"He is just being polite, children," Mr. Suárez said, and shifting his chair closer to Mr. Mendelsohn, he asked, "So . . . Mr. Mendelsohn, how you been? What's new? You okay?"

"So-so, Mr. Suárez. You know, aches and pains when you get old. But there's nothing you can do, so you gotta make the best of it."

Mr. Suárez nodded sympathetically, and they continued to talk. Mr. Mendelsohn saw the family every day, except for Mr. Suárez and Ralphy, who both worked a night shift.

Marta appeared in the entrance, holding a small child by the hand.

"There he is, Tato," she said to the child, and pointed to Mr. Mendelsohn.

"Oh, my big boy! He knows, he knows he's my best friend," Mr. Mendelsohn said, and held the brown shiny cane out toward Tato. The small boy grabbed the cane and, shrieking with delight, walked toward Mr. Mendelsohn.

"Look at that, will you?" said Ralphy. "He knows Mr. Mendelsohn better than me, his own father."

"That's because they are always together." Marta smiled. "Tato is learning to walk with his cane!"

Everyone laughed as they watched Tato climbing the old man's knee. Bending over, Mr. Mendelsohn pulled Tato onto his lap.

"Oh . . . he's getting heavy," said Mrs. Suárez. "Be careful."

"Never mind," Mr. Mendelsohn responded, hugging Tato. "That's my best boy. And look how swell he walks, and he's not even nineteen months."

"What a team," Julio said. "Tato already walks like Mr. Mendelsohn, and pretty soon he's gonna complain like him, too." Julio continued to tease the old man, who responded good-naturedly as everyone laughed.

After coffee, Mr. Mendelsohn sat on the large armchair in the living room, waiting for supper to be ready. He watched with delight as Tato walked back and forth with the cane. Mr. Mendelsohn held Tato's blanket, stuffed bear, and picture book.

"Tato," he called out, "come here. Let me read you a book—come on. I'm going to read you a nice story."

Tato climbed onto the chair and into Mr. Mendelsohn's lap. He sucked his thumb and waited. Mr. Mendelsohn opened the picture book.

"Okay. Now . . ." He pointed to the picture. "A is for Alligators. See that? Look at that big mouth and all them teeth." Tato yawned, nestled back, and closed his eyes. The old man read a few more pages and shut the book.

The soft breathing and sucking sound that Tato made assured Mr. Mendelsohn that the child was asleep. Such a smart kid. What a great boy, he said to himself. Mr. Mendelsohn was vaguely aware of a radio program, voices, and the small dog barking now and then, just before he too fell into a deep sleep.

This Sunday was very much like all the others: coffee first, then he and Tato would play a bit before napping in the large armchair. It had become a way of life for the old man. Only the High Holy Days and an occasional invitation to a family event, such as a marriage or funeral and so on, would prevent the old man from spending Sunday next door.

It had all been so effortless. No one ever asked him to leave, except late at night when he napped too long. On Saturdays, he tried to observe the Sabbath and brought in his meal. They lit the stove for him.

Mrs. Suárez was always feeding him, just like Mama. She also worried about me not eating, the old man had said to himself, pleased. At first, he had been cautious and had wondered about the food and the people that he was becoming so involved with. That first Sunday, the old man had looked suspiciously at the food they served him.

"What is it?" he had asked. Yvonne and Georgie had started giggling and looked at one another. Mrs. Suárez had responded quickly and with anger, cautioning her children, speaking to them in Spanish.

"Eat your food, Mr. Mendelsohn. You too skinny," she had told him.

"What kind of meat is it?" Mr. Mendelsohn insisted.

"It's good for you, that's what it is," Mrs. Suárez answered.

"But I—" Mr. Mendelsohn started.

"Never mind—it's good for you. I prepare everything fresh. Go ahead and eat it," Mrs. Suárez had interrupted. There was a silence as Mr. Mendelsohn sat still, not eating.

"You know, I'm not allowed to eat certain things. In my religion we have dietary laws. This is not pork or something like it, is it?"

"It's just . . . chicken. Chicken! That's what it is. It's delicious . . . and good for you," she had said with conviction.

"It doesn't look like chicken to me."

"That's because you never ate no chicken like this before. This here is—is called Puerto Rican chicken. I prepare it special. So you gonna eat it. You too skinny."

Mr. Mendelsohn had tried to protest, but Mrs. Suárez insisted. "Never mind. Now, I prepare everything clean and nice. You eat the chicken. You gonna like it. Go on!"

And that was all.

Mr. Mendelsohn ate his Sunday supper from then on without doubt or hesitation, accepting the affection and concern that Mrs. Suárez provided with each plateful.

That night in his own apartment, Mr. Mendelsohn felt uneasy. He remembered that during supper, Ralphy had mentioned that his GI loan had come through. They would be looking for a house soon, everyone agreed. Not in the Bronx; farther out, near Yonkers. It was more like the country there.

The old man tossed and turned in his bed. That's still a long way off. First, they have to find the house and everything. You don't move just like that! he said to himself. It's gonna take a while, he reasoned, putting such thoughts out of his mind.

Mr. Mendelsohn looked at his new quarters.

"I told you, didn't I? See how nice this is?" his sister Jennie said. She put down the large sack of groceries on the small table.

It was a fair-sized room with a single bed, a bureau, a wooden wardrobe closet, a table, and two chairs. A hot plate was set on a small white refrigerator and a white metal kitchen cabinet was placed alongside.

"We'll bring you whatever else you need, Louis," Jennie went on. "You'll love it here, I'm sure. There are people your own age, interested in the same things. Here—let's get started. We'll put your things away and you can get nicely settled."

Mr. Mendelsohn walked over to the window and looked out. He saw a wide avenue with cars, taxis, and buses speeding by. "Its gonna take me two buses, at least, to get back to the old neighborhood," he said.

"Why do you have to go back there?" Jennie asked quickly. "There is nobody there anymore, Louis. Everybody moved!"

"There's shul . . ."

"There's shul right here. Next door you have a large temple. Twice you were robbed over there. It's a miracle you weren't hurt! Louis, there is no reason for you to go back. There is nothing over there, nothing," Jennie said.

"The trouble all started with that rooming house next door. Those people took in all kinds . . . " He shook his head. "When the Suárez family lived there we had no problems. But nobody would talk to the landlord about those new people—only me. Nobody cared."

"That's all finished," Jennie said, looking at her watch. "Now look how nice it is here. Come on, let's get started." She began to put the groceries away in the refrigerator and cabinet.

"Leave it, Jennie," he interrupted. "Go on . . . I'll take care of it. You go on home. You are in a hurry."

"I'm only trying to help," Jennie responded.

"I know, I know. But I lived in one place for almost fifty years. So don't hurry me." He looked around the room. "And I ain't going nowhere now."

Shaking her head, Jennie said, "Look, this weekend we have a wedding, but next weekend Sara and I will come to see you. I'll call the hotel on the phone first, and they'll let you know. All right?"

"Sure." He nodded.

"That'll be good, Louis. This way you will get a chance to get settled and get acquainted with some of the other residents." Jennie kissed Mr. Mendelsohn affectionately. The old man nodded and turned away. In a moment, he heard the door open and shut.

Slowly, he walked to the sack of groceries and finished putting them away. Then, with much effort, he lifted a large suitcase onto the bed. He took out several photographs. Then he set the photographs upright, arranging them carefully on the bureau. He had pictures of his parents' wedding and of his sisters and their families. There was a photograph of his mother taken just before she died, and another one of Tato.

That picture was taken when he was about two years old, the old man said to himself. Yes, that's right, on his birthday . . . There was a party. And Tato was already talking. Such a smart kid, he thought, smiling. Last? Last when? he wondered. Time was going fast for him. He shrugged. He could hardly remember what year it was lately. Just before they moved! he remembered. That's right, they gave him the photograph of Tato. They had a nice house around Gun Hill Road someplace, and they had taken him there once. He recalled how exhausted he had been after the long trip. No one had a car, and they had had to take a train and buses. Anyway, he was glad he remembered. Now he could let them know he had moved, and tell them all about what happened to the old neighborhood. That's right, they had a telephone now. Yes, he said to himself, let me finish here, then I'll go call them. He continued to put the rest of his belongings away.

Mr. Mendelsohn sat in the lobby, holding on to his cane and a cake box. He had told the nurse at the desk that his friends were coming to pick him up this Sunday. He looked eagerly toward the revolving doors. After a short while, he saw Ralphy, Julio, and Georgie walk through into the lobby.

"Deliveries are made in the rear of the building," he heard the nurse at the desk say as they walked toward him.

"These are my friends, Mrs. Read," Mr. Mendelsohn said, standing. "They are here to take me out."

"Oh, well," said the nurse. "All right, I didn't realize. Here he is, then. He's been talking about nothing else but this visit." Mrs. Read smiled.

Ralphy nodded, then spoke to Georgie. "Get Mr. Mendelsohn's overcoat."

Quickly, Mr. Mendelsohn put on his coat, and all four left the lobby.

"Take good care of him now," they heard Mrs. Read calling. "You be a good boy now, Mr. Mendelsohn."

Outside, Mr. Mendelsohn looked at the young men and smiled.

"How's everyone?" he asked.

"Good," Julio said. "Look, that's my pickup truck from work. They let me use it sometimes when I'm off."

"That's a beautiful truck. How's everyone? Tato? How is my best friend? And Yvonne? Does she like school? And your mama and papa? . . . Marta?"

"Fine, fine. Everybody is doing great. Wait till you see them. We'll be there in a little while," said Julio. "With this truck, we'll get there in no time."

Mr. Mendelsohn sat in the kitchen and watched as Mrs. Suárez packed food into a shopping bag. Today had been a good day for the old man: he had napped in the old armchair and spent time with the children. Yvonne was so grown up, he almost had not recognized her. When Tato remembered him, Mr. Mendelsohn had been especially pleased. Shyly, he had shaken hands with the old man. Then he had taken him into his room to show Mr. Mendelsohn all his toys.

"Now, I packed a whole lotta stuff in this shopping bag for you. You gotta eat it. Eat some of my Puerto Rican chicken—it's good for you. You too skinny. You got enough for tomorrow and for another day. You put it in the refrigerator. Also I put some rice and other things."

He smiled as she spoke, enjoying the attention he received.

"Julio is gonna drive you back before it gets too late," she said. "And we gonna pick you up again and bring you back to eat with us. I bet you don't eat right." She shook her head. "Okay?"

"You shouldn't go through so much bother," he protested mildly.

"Again with the bother? You stop that! We gonna see you soon. You take care of yourself and eat. Eat! You must nourish yourself, especially in such cold weather."

Mr. Mendelsohn and Mrs. Suárez walked out into the living room. The family exchanged goodbyes with the old man. Tato, feeling less shy, kissed Mr. Mendelsohn on the cheek.

Just before leaving, Mr. Mendelsohn embraced Mrs. Suárez for a long time, as everybody watched silently.

"Thank you," he whispered.

"Thank you? For what?" Mrs. Suárez said. "You come back soon and have Sunday supper with us. Yes?" Mr. Mendelsohn nodded and smiled.

It was dark and cold out. He walked with effort. Julio carried the shopping bag. Slowly, he got into the pickup truck. The ride back was bumpy and uncomfortable for Mr. Mendelsohn. The cold wind cut right through into the truck, and the old man was aware of the long winter ahead.

His eyelids were so heavy he could hardly open them. Nurses scurried about busily. Mr. Mendelsohn heard voices.

"Let's give him another injection. It will help his breathing. Nurse! Nurse! The patient needs . . ."

The voices faded. He remembered he had gone to sleep after supper last—last when? How many days have I been here . . . here in the hospital? Yes, he thought, now I know where I am. A heart attack, the doctor had said, and then he had felt even worse. Didn't matter; I'm too tired. He heard voices once more, and again he barely opened his eyes. A tall thin man dressed in white spoke to him.

"Mr. Mendelsohn, can you hear me? How do you feel now? More comfortable? We called your family. I spoke to your sister, Mrs. Wiletsky. They should be here very soon. You feeling sleepy? Good. Take a little nap—go on. We'll wake you when they get here, don't worry. Go on now."

He closed his eyes, thinking of Jennie. She'll be here soon with Esther and Rosalie and Sara. All of them. He smiled. He was so tired. His bed was by the window and a bright warm sash of sunshine covered him almost completely. Nice and warm, he thought, and felt comfortable. The pain had lessened, practically disappeared. Mr. Mendelsohn heard the birds chirping and Sporty barking. That's all right, Mrs. Suárez would let him sleep. She wouldn't wake him up, he knew that. It looked like a good warm day; he planned to take Tato out for a walk later. That's some smart kid, he thought. Right now he was going to rest.

"This will be the last of it, Sara."

"Just a few more things, Jennie, and we'll be out of here." The two women spoke as they packed away all the items in the room. They opened drawers and cabinets, putting things away in boxes and suitcases.

"What about these pictures on the bureau?" asked Sara.

Jennie walked over and they both looked at the photographs.

"There's Mama and Papa's wedding picture. Look, there's you, Sara, when Jonathan was born. And Esther and . . . look, he's got all the pictures of the entire family." Jennie burst into tears.

"Come on, Jennie. It's all over, honey. He was sick and very old." The older woman comforted the younger one.

Wiping her eyes, Jennie said, "Well, we did the best we could for him, anyway."

"Who is this?" asked Sara, holding up Tato's photo.

"Let me see," said Jennie. "Hummm . . . that must be one of the people in that family that lived next door in the old apartment on Prospect Avenue. You know—remember that Spanish family? He used to visit with them. Their name was . . . Díaz or something like that, I think. I can't remember."

"Oh yes," said Sara. "Louis mentioned them once in a while, yes. They were nice to him. What shall we do with it? Return it?"

"Oh," said Jennie, "that might be rude. What do you think?"

"Well, I don't want it, do you?"

"No." Jennie hesitated. "But let's just put it away. Maybe we ought to tell them what happened. About Louis." Sara shrugged her shoulders. "Maybe I'll write to them," Jennie went on, "if I can find out where they live. They moved. What do you say?"

The Force of Luck

Rudolfo A. Anaya

ONCE two wealthy friends got into a heated argument. One said that it was money which made a man prosperous, and the other maintained that it wasn't money, but luck, which made the man. They argued for some time and finally decided that if only they could find an honorable man then perhaps they could prove their respective points of view.

One day while they were passing through a small village they came upon a miller who was grinding corn and wheat. They paused to ask the man how he ran his business. The miller replied that he worked for a master and that he earned only four bits a day, and with that he had to support a family of five.

The friends were surprised. "Do you mean to tell us you can maintain a family of five on only fifteen dollars a month?" one asked.

"I live modestly to make ends meet," the humble miller replied.

The two friends privately agreed that if they put this man to a test perhaps they could resolve their argument.

"I am going to make you an offer," one of them said to the miller. "I will give you two hundred dollars and you may do whatever you want with the money."

"But why would you give me this money when you've just met me?" the miller asked.

"Well, my good man, my friend and I have a long standing argument. He contends that it is luck which elevates a man to high position, and I say it is money. By giving you this money perhaps we can settle our argument. Here, take it, and do with it what you want!"

So the poor miller took the money and spent the rest of the day thinking about the strange meeting which had presented him with more money than he had ever seen. What could he possibly do with all this money? Be that as it may, he had the money in his pocket and he could do with it whatever he wanted.

When the day's work was done, the miller decided the first thing he would do would be to buy food for his family. He took out ten dollars and wrapped the rest of the money in a cloth and put the bundle in his bag. Then he went to the market and bought supplies and a good piece of meat to take home.

On the way home he was attacked by a hawk that had smelled the meat which the miller carried. The miller fought off the bird but in the struggle he lost the bundle of money. Before the miller knew what was happening the hawk grabbed the bag and flew away with it. When he realized what had happened he fell into deep thought.

"Ah," he moaned, "wouldn't it have been better to let that hungry bird have the meat! I could have bought a lot more meat with the money he took. Alas, now I'm in the same poverty as before! And worse, because now those two men will say I am a thief! I should have thought carefully and bought nothing. Yes, I should have gone straight home and this wouldn't have happened!"

So he gathered what was left of his provisions and continued home, and when he arrived he told his family the entire story.

When he was finished telling his story his wife said, "It has been our lot to be poor, but have faith in God and maybe someday our luck will change."

The next day the miller got up and went to work as usual. He wondered what the two men would say about his story. But since he had never been a man of money he soon forgot the entire matter.

Three months after he had lost the money to the hawk, it happened that the two wealthy men returned to the village. As soon as they saw the miller they approached him to ask if his luck had changed. When the miller saw them he felt ashamed and afraid that they would think that he had squandered the money on worthless things. But he decided to tell them the truth and as soon as they had greeted each other he told his story. The men believed him. In fact, the one who insisted that it was money and not luck which made a man prosper took out another two hundred dollars and gave it to the miller.

"Let's try again," he said, "and let's see what happens this time."

The miller didn't know what to think. "Kind sir, maybe it would be better if you put this money in the hands of another man," he said.

"No," the man insisted, "I want to give it to you because you are an honest man, and if we are going to settle our argument you have to take the money!"

The miller thanked them and promised to do his best. Then as soon as the two men left he began to think what to do with the money so that it wouldn't disappear as it had the first time. The thing to do was to take the money straight home. He took out ten dollars, wrapped the rest in a cloth, and headed home.

When he arrived his wife wasn't at home. At first he didn't know what to do with the money. He went to the pantry where he had stored a large earthenware jar filled with bran. That was as safe a place as any to hide the money, he thought, so he emptied out the grain and put the bundle of money at the bottom of the jar, then covered it up with the grain. Satisfied that the money was safe he returned to work.

That afternoon when he arrived home from work he was greeted by his wife.

"Look, my husband, today I bought some good clay with which to whitewash the entire house."

"And how did you buy the clay if we don't have any money?" he asked.

"Well, the man who was selling the clay was willing to trade for jewelry, money, or anything of value," she said. "The only thing we had of value was the jar full of bran, so I traded it for the clay. Isn't it wonderful, I think we have enough clay to whitewash these two rooms!"

The man groaned and pulled his hair.

"Oh, you crazy woman! What have you done? We're ruined again!"

"But why?" she asked, unable to understand his anguish.

"Today I met the same two friends who gave me the two hundred dollars three months ago," he explained. "And after I told them how I lost the money they gave me another two hundred. And I, to make sure the money was safe, came home and hid it inside the jar of bran—the same jar you have traded for dirt! Now we're as poor as we were before! And what am I going to tell the two men? They'll think I'm a liar and a thief for sure!"

"Let them think what they want," his wife said calmly. "We will only have in our lives what the good Lord wants us to have. It is our lot to be poor until God wills it otherwise."

So the miller was consoled and the next day he went to work as usual. Time came and went, and one day the two wealthy friends returned to ask the miller how he had done with the second two hundred dollars. When the poor miller saw them he was afraid they would accuse him of being a liar and a spendthrift. But he decided to be truthful and as soon as they had greeted each other he told them what had happened to the money.

The Force of Luck

"That is why poor men remain honest," the man who had given him the money said, "Because they don't have money they can't get into trouble. But I find your stories hard to believe. I think you gambled and lost the money. That's why you're telling us these wild stories."

"Either way," he continued, "I still believe that it is money and not luck which makes a man prosper."

"Well, you certainly didn't prove your point by giving the money to this poor miller," his friend reminded him. "Good evening, you luckless man," he said to the miller.

"Thank you, friends," the miller said.

"Oh, by the way, here is a worthless piece of lead I've been carrying around. Maybe you can use it for something," said the man who believed in luck. Then the two men left, still debating their points of view on life.

Since the lead was practically worthless, the miller thought nothing of it and put it in his jacket pocket. He forgot all about it until he arrived home. When he threw his jacket on a chair he heard a thump and he remembered the piece of lead. He took it out of the pocket and threw it under the table. Later that night after the family had eaten and gone to bed, they heard a knock at the door.

"Who is it? What do you want?" the miller asked.

"It's me, your neighbor," a voice answered. The miller recognized the fisherman's wife. "My husband sent me to ask you if you have any lead you can spare. He is going fishing tomorrow and he needs the lead to weight down the nets."

The miller remembered the lead he had thrown under the table. He got up, found it, and gave it to the woman.

"Thank you very much, neighbor," the woman said, "I promise you the first fish my husband catches will be yours."

"Think nothing of it," the miller said and returned to bed. The next day he got up and went to work without thinking any more of the incident. But in the afternoon when he returned home he found his wife cooking a big fish for dinner.

"Since when are we so well off we can afford fish for supper?" he asked his wife.

"Don't you remember that our neighbor promised us the first fish her husband caught?" his wife reminded him. "Well this was the fish he caught the first time he threw his net. So it's ours, and it's a beauty. But you should have been here when I gutted him! I found a large piece of glass in his stomach!"

"And what did you do with it?"

"Oh, I gave it to the children to play with," she shrugged.

When the miller saw the piece of glass he noticed it shone so brightly it appeared to illuminate the room, but because he knew nothing about jewels he didn't realize its value and left it to the children. But the bright glass was such a novelty that the children were soon fighting over it and raising a terrible fuss.

Now it so happened that the miller and his wife had other neighbors who were jewelers. The following morning when the miller had gone to work the jeweler's wife visited the miller's wife to complain about all the noise her children had made.

"We couldn't get any sleep last night," she moaned.

"I know, and I'm sorry, but you know how it is with a large family," the miller's wife explained. "Yesterday we found a beautiful piece of glass and I gave it to my youngest one to play with and when the others tried to take it from him he raised a storm."

The jeweler's wife took interest. "Won't you show me that piece of glass?" she asked.

"But of course. Here it is."

"Ah, yes, it's a pretty piece of glass. Where did you find it?"

"Our neighbor gave us a fish yesterday and when I was cleaning it I found the glass in its stomach."

"Why don't you let me take it home for just a moment. You see, I have one just like it and I want to compare them."

"Yes, why not? Take it," answered the miller's wife.

So the jeweler's wife ran off with the glass to show it to her husband. When the jeweler saw the glass he instantly knew it was one of the finest diamonds he had ever seen.

"It's a diamond!" he exclaimed.

"I thought so," his wife nodded eagerly. "What shall we do?"

"Go tell the neighbor we'll give her fifty dollars for it, but don't tell her it's a diamond!"

"No, no," his wife chuckled, "of course not." She ran to her neighbor's house. "Ah yes, we have one exactly like this," she told the miller's wife. "My husband is willing to buy it for fifty dollars—only so we can have a pair, you understand."

"I can't sell it," the miller's wife answered. "You will have to wait until my husband returns from work."

That evening when the miller came home from work his wife told him about the offer the jeweler had made for the piece of glass.

"But why would they offer fifty dollars for a worthless piece of glass?" the miller wondered aloud. Before his wife could answer they were interrupted by the jeweler's wife.

"What do you say, neighbor, will you take fifty dollars for the glass?" she asked.

"No, that's not enough," the miller said cautiously. "Offer more."

"I'll give you fifty thousand!" the jeweler's wife blurted out.

"A little bit more," the miller replied.

"Impossible!" the jeweler's wife cried, "I can't offer any more without consulting my husband." She ran off to tell her husband how the bartering was going, and he told her he was prepared to pay a hundred thousand dollars to acquire the diamond.

He handed her seventy-five thousand dollars and said, "Take this and tell him that tomorrow, as soon as I open my shop, he'll have the rest."

When the miller heard the offer and saw the money he couldn't believe his eyes. He imagined the jeweler's wife was jesting with him, but it was a true offer and he received the hundred thousand dollars for the diamond. The miller had never seen so much money, but he still didn't quite trust the jeweler.

"I don't know about this money," he confided to his wife. "Maybe the jeweler plans to accuse us of robbing him and thus get it back."

"Oh no," his wife assured him, "the money is ours. We sold the diamond fair and square—we didn't rob anyone."

"I think I'll still go to work tomorrow," the miller said. "Who knows, something might happen and the money will disappear, then we would be without money and work. Then how would we live?"

So he went to work the next day, and all day he thought about how he could use the money. When he returned home that afternoon his wife asked him what he had decided to do with their new fortune.

"I think I will start my own mill," he answered, "like the one I operate for my master. Once I set up my business we'll see how our luck changes."

The next day he set about buying everything he needed to establish his mill and to build a new home. Soon he had everything going.

Six months had passed, more or less, since he had seen the two men who had given him the four hundred dollars and the piece of lead. He was eager to see them again and to tell them how the piece of lead had changed his luck and made him wealthy.

Time passed and the miller prospered. His business grew and he even built a summer cottage where he could take his family on vacation. He had many employees who worked for him. One day while he was at his store he saw his two benefactors riding by. He rushed out into the street to greet them and asked them to come in. He was overjoyed to see them, and he was happy to see that they admired his store.

"Tell us the truth," the man who had given him the four hundred dollars said, "You used that money to set up this business."

The miller swore he hadn't, and he told them how he had given the piece of lead to his neighbor and how the fisherman had in return given him a fish with a very large diamond in its stomach. And he told them how he had sold the diamond.

"And that's how I acquired this business and many other things I want to show you," he said. "But it's time to eat. Let's eat first then I'll show you everything I have now."

The men agreed, but one of them still doubted the miller's story. So they ate and then the miller had three horses saddled and they rode out to see his summer home. The cabin was on the other side of the river where the mountains were cool and beautiful. When they arrived the men admired the place very much. It was such a peaceful place that they rode all afternoon through the forest. During their ride they came upon a tall pine tree.

"What is that on top of the tree?" one of them asked.

"That's the nest of a hawk," the miller replied.

"I have never seen one; I would like to take a closer look at it!"

"Of course," the miller said, and he ordered a servant to climb the tree and bring down the nest so his friend could see how it was built. When the hawk's nest was on the ground they examined it carefully. They noticed that there was a cloth bag at the bottom of the nest. When the miller saw the bag he immediately knew that it was the very same bag he had lost to the hawk which fought him for the piece of meat years ago.

"You won't believe me, friends, but this is the very same bag in which I put the first two hundred dollars you gave me," he told them.

"If it's the same bag," the man who had doubted him said, "then the money you said the hawk took should be there."

"No doubt about that," the miller said. "Let's see what we find."

The three of them examined the old, weatherbeaten bag. Although it was full of holes and crumbling, when they tore it apart they found the money intact. The two men remembered what the miller had told them and they agreed he was an honest and honorable man. Still, the man who had given him the money wasn't satisfied. He wondered what had really happened to the second two hundred he had given the miller.

They spent the rest of the day riding in the mountains and returned very late to the house.

As he unsaddled their horses, the servant in charge of grooming and feeding the horses suddenly realized that he had no grain for them. He ran to the barn and checked, but there was no grain for the hungry horses. So he ran to the neighbor's granary and there he was able to buy a large clay jar of bran. He carried the jar home and emptied the bran into a bucket to wet it before he fed it to the horses. When he got to the bottom of the jar he noticed a large lump which turned out to be a rag covered package. He examined it and felt something inside. He immediately went to give it to his master who had been eating dinner.

"Master," he said, "look at this package which I found in an earthenware jar of grain which I just bought from our neighbor!"

The three men carefully unraveled the cloth and found the other one hundred and ninety dollars which the miller had told them he had lost. That is how the miller proved to his friends that he was truly an honest man.

And they had to decide for themselves whether it had been luck or money which had made the miller a wealthy man!

La suerte

José Griego y Maestas

ESTOS eran dos compañeros que andaban en una porfía, uno decía que el dinero levantaba al hombre y el otro sostenía que no era el dinero, sino la suerte. Aunduvieron porfiando mucho tiempo con deseos de encontrar un hombre honrado para poder probar sus puntos de vista.

Tocó la casualidad un día que pasando por una plaza se encontraron con un molinero que estaba moliendo maíz y trigo. Se dirigieron a donde estaba el hombre para preguntarle cómo corría su negocio. El hombre les respondió muy atentamente que el trabajaba por otro señor y que ganaba solamente cuatro reales al día, con lo que mantenía a su familia de cinco.

"Y usted, ¿se acabala con quince pesos al mes para mantener a su familia de cinco?"

"Pues me limito todo lo que puedo para mantener a mi familia, no porque tengo suficiente."

"Pues entonces le voy a hacer un presente. Aquí le voy a regalar doscientos pesos para ver lo que va a determinar hacer con ellos."

"No, señor" le dijo el hombre, "no creo que usted me pueda regalar ese dinero la primera vez que yo lo miro a usted."

"Señor" le dijo él, "yo le voy a dejar este dinero a usted porque yo y este hombre porfiamos. El porfía que la suerte es la que levanta al hombre y yo digo que el dinero es el que levanta."

Cuando el hombre pobre tomó el dinero, pasó todo el día reflexionando sobre aquel negocio. ¿Qué podría hacer con todo el dinero? Aquel hombre se lo dio para calarlo, y él podría determinar del dinero como si fuera suyo. Sea como fuere, él tenía el dinero en su bolsa e iba a determinar de ello como le pareciere.

Se llegó la hora de salir del trabajo y se fue él con su dinero a comprar algunas provisiones para su familia. Tomó diez pesos y envolvió los ciento noventa restantes en unos trapos y en una blusa de lona que traiba. Cuando llegó a la plaza, trató bastantes negocios allí y compró un buen pedazo de carne para llevarle a su familia.

En el camino a sue casa, al olor de la carne, le salió un gavilán hambriento. El hombre se puso a pelear con el gavilán; el animal andaba tras de la carne y el hombre se defendía. En el reborujo con el gavilán, se le cayó la blusa en donde llevaba la cantidad de dinero. El gavilán agarró la blusa y se la llevó. Cuando el hombre reparó que el gavilán se llevó su blusa, se rascó la cabeza y pensó:

"¡Cuánto más valía haberle dejado a este hambriento animal que se llevara el pedazo de carne! Cuántos más pedazos de carne hubiera comprado yo con el dinero que se llevó. ¡Ahora voy a quedar en la misma calamidad que antes! Y antes más ahora, porque estos hombres me van a juzgar por un ladrón. Tal vez si yo hubiera pensado diferente en mi negocio, no debía de haber comprado nada; haberme venido para mi casa para que no me hubiera pasado una cosa semejante."

De todos modos siguió el hombre con la provisión que le había quedado para su familia. Cuando llegó a su casa, le platicó a su familia lo que le había pasado.

"De cualquier modo," le dijo su esposa, "nos ha tocado ser pobres. Pero ten fe en Dios, que algún día nuestra suerte cambiara."

Otro día en la mañana se levantó este hombre como de costumbre y se fue a su trabajo. Todo el día estuvo pensando en lo que había pasado y en lo que aquellos hombres juzgarían tocante a lo que él les iba a reportar. De todos modos, como él nunca había sido hombre dueño de dinero, pronto se le olvidó este negocio de los doscientos pesos.

Después de pasados tres meses desde que le había quitado el bellaco animal su dinero, tocó la casualidad que volvieron los mismos hombres. Tan pronto como vieron al molinero, se dirigieron a donde él estaba para que les informara cómo lo había tratado la suerte. Tan pronto como él los vido, se puso muy avergonzado. Temía que estos hombres pensaran que él podía haber malgastado aquel dinero en cosas que no habían sido buenas, ni para él ni para su familia. Cuando estos hombres lo saludaron él les contestó también con mucho agrado y al mismo tiempo les refirió tal como le había pasado. Siempre estos hombres quedaron conformes y el que alegaba que el dinero levantaba al hombre, volvió a sacar doscientos pesos de su bolsa y se los volvió a regalar a este señor. Le deseó que le fuera poco mejor que la primera vez. No hallaba qué pensar este hombre cuando volvió a recibir otra vez doscientos pesos, y dijo al que se los dio:

"Señor, valía más que usted pusiera este dinero en manos de otro hombre."

"Pues mi gusto es dejártelos a ti, porque me pareces ser un hombre honrado. Tú tienes que quedarte con el dinero."

Le dio repetidas gracias y prometió hacer lo mejor que él pudiera. Tan pronto como estos hombres se despidieron, se puso a reflexionar qué hacer con el dinero para no tener ningún inconveniente en el cual se pudiera desperdiciar sin haberlo usado. Pensó inmediatamente ir a llevar el dinero a su propia casa. Tomó diez pesos y envolvió ciento noventa en unos trapos y se fue para su casa.

Cuando llegó a su casa no encontró a su esposa. Viendo que la casa estaba sola no hallaba dónde poner el dinero. Se fue a la despensa donde tenían una tinaja llena de salvado, vació el salvado de la tinaja y puso el dinero al fondo de la tinaja envuelto tal como estaba y volvió a echar el salvado arriba del dinero. Se salió apresuradamente a su trabajo sin haberle dado cuenta a nadie.

Cuando vino en la tarde de su trabajo, su esposa le dijo:

"¡Mira, hijo! Yo compré una poca de tierra para enjarrar la casa por dentro."

"Y ¿con qué has mercado tierra, si no tenemos dinero?"

"Sí," le dice la mujer, "pero este hombre andaba vendiendo la tierra, fuera por prendas, dinero, o cualquiera cosa. La única cosa de valor que teníamos para feriar era la tinaja de salvado, así que le di la tinaja de salvado por la tierra. Creo que será suficiente para que yo enjarre estos dos cuartos."

Se jaló de los cabellos el hombre y le interrumpió a la mujer:

"¡Ay, mujer bárbara! ¿Qué has hecho? ¡Otra vez nos quedamos en la ruina! Habías de haber visto que hoy mismo me encontré con los mismos amigos que me habían dado los doscientos pesos tres meses pasados y, habiéndoles platicado cómo perdí el dinero, me volvieron a regalar doscientos pesos más, y yo, por tenerlos más seguros, los eché dentro de la olla del salvado, ¿Qué es lo que voy a reportarle a estos hombres ahora? Ahora acabarán de juzgar que yo soy un ladrón."

"Que piensen como quieran," dijo la mujer "que al cabo uno no tiene más que lo que Dios quiere. Ya nos tocó ser pobres. Sólo Dios sabrá hasta cuándo."

Otro día en la mañana se levantó como de costumbre y se fue a su trabajo.

Yendo y viniendo el tiempo volvieron estos hombres a donde estaba el molinero en su negocio para informarse de lo que le había pasado esta segunda vez con el dinero. Cuando el pobre los vido venir a donde estaba él, no dejó de avergonzarse y creer que estos hombres juzgaban que él era un traidor y que estaba malgastando el dinero. Tan pronto como llegaron a donde estaba él, se saludaron, y el molinero trató de hacerles saber lo que le había pasado esta vez con el segundo dinero que le habían presentado. El hombre que le había dado el dinero se sintió mal y le dijo que asina eran muchos hombres pobres, que eran muy honestos y muy honrados solamente porque no tenían dinero para andar en otras bromas. Pero como él había recibido dinero, probablemente se había dedicado a juegos, y asina es como había gastado el dinero y ahora le salía con ese cuento.

"Sea como sea," dijo el hombre, "yo todavía sostengo que los hombres se levantan a fuerza de dinero y no por la suerte."

"Bueno, entonces pase usted muy buenas tardes."

"Muy bien, amigo."

"Tenga, aquí está un pedazo de plomo. Pueda que para alguna cosa le sirva," le dijo el que sostenía que la suerte era la que levantaba a los hombres y no el dinero.

Como ésta no era una cosa de valor, la recibió y se la echó en la bolsa de su chaqueta. En la tarde cuando llegó a su casa, tiró su chaqueta arriba de una silleta y oyó alguna cosa sonar. Se acordó del pedazo de plomo que le había regalado este individuo, lo sacó de la bolsa y lo tiró asina como para abajo de una mesa. No volvió a hacer más recuerdo del pedazo de plomo. Cenaron él y toda su familia. Después de que cenaron, se acostaron. No más en cuanto se acabaron de acostar, sonaron la puerta.

"¿Quién es? "¿Qué se ofrece?"

"Yo, vecino. Dice su vecino que si no tiene un pedazo de plomo por ahí guardado por casualidad. Que le haga favor, si tiene, de darle un poco, que mañana tiene que hacer una pesca muy grande y no tiene suficiente plomo para componer sus redes."

En eso se acordó el hombre de que había tirado el pedazo de plomo para abajo de la mesa. Se levantó y lo buscó y se lo entregó a la mujer.

"Muy bien, vecino, muchísimas gracias. Le prometo que el primer pescado que pesque su vecino, ha de ser para usted."

Se levantó muy de mañana el hombre y se fue a su trabajo sin haber reflexionado más sobre el pedazo de plomo.

En la tarde cuando vino a la casa, encontró que tenían un pescado muy grande para cenar.

"¿De dónde, hija, estamos tan bien nosotros que vamos a cenar pescado?"

"¿No te acuerdas que anoche nos prometió la vecina que el primer pescado que pescara el vecino nos lo iba a regalar a nosotros? Este fue el único pescado que pescó en la primera vez que echó la red. ¡Y si vieras hijo! ¡Lo que más me almira, que este pescado tenía adentro un pedazo de vidrio muy grande!"

"Y ¿qué hiciste con él?"

"Se lo di a los muchachos para que jugaran con él."

Fueron a ver el pedazo de vidrio que tenían los muchachitos. El vidrio iluminaba el cuarto obscuro. El hombre y la mujer no sabían lo que eran diamantes, así que no se fijaron en guardar el vidrio, sino que se lo dejaron a los muchachos para que jugaran con él. Por la novedad del vidrio los muchachos empezaron a pelear por él. Los más grandes se lo quitaban al más chiquito, por donde el chiquito hacía una bulla terrible.

Estos pobres tenían unos vecinos judíos que eran joyeros. En la mañana se levantó el hombre y se fue al trabajo. La mujer del joyero llegó después para pedirle a la mujer del molinero que tuviera más cuidado de su familia porque estaban haciendo mucha bulla los niños, y no los dejaban dormir.

"Sí, vecina, es verdad lo que usted dice. Pero ya ve cómo es donde hay familia. Pues usted verá que ayer hallamos un vidrio y se lo di al niño más chiquito para que jugara con él y cuando los más grandes se lo quieren quitar, él forma un escándalo grande."

"¡A ver!" le dijo la mujer. "¿Por qué no me enseña ese vidrio?"

"Sí se lo puedo enseñar. Aquí está."

"Qué bonito vidrio es éste. ¿Dónde lo hallaron?"

"Pues adentro de un pescado. Ayer estaba limpiando un pescado y el vidrio estaba adentro de él."

"Empréstemelo para llevarlo a mi casa para ver si se parece a uno que tengo."

"Sí," le dice. "¿Por qué no? Llévelo."

Se llevó la vecina el vidrio a enseñárselo al marido. Cuando el joyero miró este vidrio, vido que era de los diamentes más finos que jamás había visto.

"Este es un diamante," le dice a su esposa. "Anda, dile a la vecina que le damos cincuenta pesos por él."

Fue la esposa del joyero con el vidrio en la mano y le dice a la vecina:

"Dice su vecino que si quiere, que le damos cincuenta pesos por este vidrio. Todo lo hacemos porque es muy parecido a otro que tenemos nosotros y asina podíamos hacer un par muy bonito."

"De ningún modo, vecina, puedo yo vendérselo. Eso puede hacerse a la tarde cuando venga mi esposo."

En la tarde cuando vino el molinero del trabajo, le contó su esposa lo que había ofrecido su vecino el joyero. En esto estaban hablando cuando entró la mujer del joyero.

"¿Qué dice, vecino, quiere cincuenta pesos por el vidrio?"

"Alárguese poco más."

"Le daré cincuenta mil pesos."

"Poco más." le dice.

"No puedo alargarme más. Voy a ver a mi esposo a ver qué me dice. Hasta ahí no más me dijo que me alargara."

Fue la esposa del joyero y le dijo a su esposo lo que había reportado el vecino. El joyero entonces sacó setenta y cinco mil pesos y le dijo:

"Llévale estos y dile que mañana, luego que se abra allá, le traeré lo restante, que le voy a dar cien mil pesos."

Cuando el molinero vido a la mujer con aquel dineral, cuasi no lo creía él. Creía que aquella mujer estaba chanceándose. Pero sea como fuere, el pobre recibió cien mil pesos por el diamante.

Cuando el molinero se vido con tanto dinero, él y su esposa no hallaban qué pensar. Decía él:

"Pues no sé de este dinero; el joyero de repente nos podía levantar un crimen que nosotros lo hemos robado, o de alguna manera nos podía levantar un perjuicio muy grande."

"¡Oh, no!" decía la mujer. "Ese dinero es de nosotros. Nosotros vendimos el vidrio por ese dinero. Nosotros no se lo robamos a nadien."

"De todos modos yo voy mañana a trabajar, hija. No nos vaya a suceder que se nos acabe el dinero y no tengamos ni el dinero ni el trabajo y entonces, ¿cómo nos vamos a mantener?"

Se fue el hombre al otro día a su trabajo. Todo el día se estuvo pensando y pensando cómo podía dirigir aquel dinero para que le cambiara su suerte. En la tarde cuando volvió del trabajo, le dijo su esposa:

"¿Qué has dicho o qué has pensado? ¿Qué vas a determinar hacer con este dineral que tenemos?"

"Voy a ver si puedo poner un molino, tal como el que yo estoy corriendo de mi amo. Quiero poner un comercio y asina, poco a poco, veremos si cambiamos nuestra suerte."

Otro día este hombre se fue con mucho empeño y anduvo negociando, comprando todo lo necesario para poner un molino, un comercio, y una casa. Pronto arregló todo.

Ya pasaban como unos seis meses, tal vez más, desde que no había visto a los hombres que le regalaron los cuatrocientos pesos y el pedazo de plomo. El tenía muchos deseos de verlos, para hacerles saber cuánto le había ayudado aquel pedazo de plomo que le regaló el hombre que reclamaba que la suerte era la que ayudaba al hombre a levantarse y no el dinero.

Yendo y viniendo el tiempo, el molinero estaba muy bien puesto. Tenía muy buen comercio, había levantado una casa de campo adonde irse a divertir con su familia, y tenía criados que trabajaban por él.

Un día que estaba en su tienda, vio pasar aquellos dos señores que más antes le habían regalado cuatrocientos pesos y el pedazo de plomo. Tan pronto como los vido, salió a la calle a encontrarlos y a suplicarles que le hicieran el favor de entrar para dentro. El tenía mucho gusto de hablar con ellos y verlos. Tan pronto como entraron, aquellos hombres quedaron admirados de ver aquella tienda tan grande que él tenía. Al mismo tiempo el que le había regalado los cuatrocientos pesos no dejaba de juzgar que éste hombre había empleado aquel dinero en este comercio, pera a él se lo negaba. El molinero les platicó cómo había dado el pedazo de plomo a su vecino y luego cómo el pescador le había regalado un pescado que tenía adentro un diamante muy grande. Les contó también de la venta del diamante por una cantidad de dinero enorme y terminó diciéndoles:

"Y asina es como he adquirido este comercio y muchas otras cosas que quiero enseñarles. Pero ya es hora de comer. Vamos a tomar la comida y luego vamos a tomar un paseo para enseñarles todo lo que tengo."

Tomaron la comida y luego que acabaron de comer mandó a un muchacho que ensillara tres caballos, y se fueron los tres a pasearse para enseñarles la casa de campo que tenía. Esta casa de campo estaba al otro lado del río donde había bastante monte en un lugar muy bonito. Cuando llegaron allá, les gustó mucho el lugar a los hombres y empezaron a pasearse entre el monte. Durante su paseo le llamó la atención a uno de los hombres un nido de gavilán que estaba allá arriba en un pinabete.

"Y eso que se ve allá arriba, ¿qué cosa es?"

"Eso es un nido de gavilán,"dijo el dueño del rancho.

"¡Cómo desearía ver yo ese nido más cerquita!"

En eso mandó el hombre a uno de sus criados que subiera arriba del pinabete y bajara el nido con cuidado para satisfacerle a su amigo el deseo que tenía de ver aquel nido más cerquita. Cuando el nido estaba abajo lo estuvieron examinando los tres hombres muy bien y entonces notaron que abajo del nido estaba como una blusa de lona. Cuando el molinero vido la blusa, de una vez reflexionó que era la lona que él traiba puesta cuando el gavilán hambriento había peleado con él por el pedazo de carne, y no habiéndole podido quitar la carne, se había llevado la blusa entre las uñas.

"¿Qué no les parece, amigos, que esta es la blusa que tenía yo el día que me regalaron los primeros doscientos pesos?"

"Pues si es esta la misma blusa," dijo él, "que tenías cuando te regalamos el dinero, aquí han de estar los doscientos que tú nos reportaste que el gavilán se había robado con todo y blusa."

"Pues creo que no hay duda. Esta es mi blusa y vamos a examinar a ver qué es lo qué hallamos."

Empezaron entre los tres amigos a examinar la blusa. Aunque la blusa tenía bastantes agujeros por estar apolillada, encontraron que el lugar donde había puesto el dinero no había sido afectado de ningún modo, y el dinero estaba perfectamente tal como él había reportado. Los dos hombres confesaron lo que el molinero les había dicho más antes y juzgaron que era un hombre honesto y honrado. Pero el hombre que le había hecho los presentes de dinero no quedaba muy satisfecho porque no había encontrado los otros ciento noventa que faltaban.

Pasaron el día muy contentos, paseándose, y ya se vinieron poco tarde a la casa. El hombre que atendía a los caballos no se había dado cuenta de que no había grano para los caballos cuando volvieran. Y en eso que llegaron, fue al comercio de ellos mismos y no encontró grano para darles a los caballos que habían llegado. Se fue a otro comercio que estaba inmediato y allá encontró que no había más que un tinaja de salvado. Trujo la tinaja de salvado y cuando llegó a la casa de su amo vació el salvado en otra cubeta para mojarlo y dárselo a los caballos. Al vaciar la tinaja notó que estaba un bulto algo grande como un empaque envuelto en unos trapos en el fondo de la tinaja. Lo cogió, lo examinó y vido que alguna cosa contenía. Hizo por quitarle bien el salvado para que quedara limpio y fue a presentarlo a su amo que estaba cenando.

"Mi señor, mire qué bulto he encontrado dentro de una tinaja que he comprado al otro comerciante."

"¿Qué es lo que hablas de tinaja?"

"Sí," le dijo, "que he hallado este envoltorio dentro de una tinaja llena de salvado."

Lo tomaron y los tres hombres allí mismo curiosamente estuvieron desenvolviendo con muy buen cuidado los trapos y descubrieron que allí estaban los otros ciento noventa que el molinero les había dicho que había perdido. Y aquí acabó de probar el molinero a sus amigos que él había tratado siempre con la verdad y que él no estaba mintiéndoles.

Y se pusieron a reflejar si era el dinero o la suerte lo que le ayudó al molinero levantarse.

The Lost Camel

Rudolfo A. Anaya

THERE were once some merchants from across the ocean who traveled from place to place selling their wares. Late one evening as they made their way up the Río Grande they lost one of their camels. They discovered he was missing when they stopped to make camp that night.

Early the next morning when they set out to look for him they met a man coming along the road. They stopped and asked him if he had seen a camel. The man told them that he had not seen the camel, but he was sure he could tell them where the camel was to be found.

The merchants were puzzled by this, and began to question the man. "Was the camel carrying a load?" they asked.

"Yes," the man answered. "He was carrying bags of wheat on his left side and a large jug of honey on his right side. Furthermore, the camel is blind in one eye and he has a missing tooth. But like I said, I haven't seen him. I can only tell you where you can find him."

"But you have given a perfect description of our lost camel!" the surprised merchants exclaimed. "You probably have hidden our camel and intend to steal him!"

"I haven't seen him and I'm not a thief!" the man retorted. "But I have lived in this land a long time and there are some things I know!"

"Then tell us, how do you know he was carrying wheat and honey?" the merchants asked suspiciously.

"I know he was carrying wheat on his left side because grains had fallen along the left side of the path. The bag was probably cut by some branches. Ants were gathering the grains on the left side of the trail. I know he was carrying jars of honey because on the right side of the path flies were swarming where the honey had dripped."

"Fine, but how do you know he is blind in one eye?" the merchants asked.

"Because I noticed he had been grazing only on the right side of the path," the man answered.

"And how do you know he has a tooth missing?"

"Because where he had chewed the grass he left a clump in the middle of the bite. That told me he had a tooth missing."

"If the directions you give us are correct," the merchants said, "then we will reward you for the good news you have given us."

And so they went off to look for the camel, and they found him near the place where the man said he had seen the signs. They were very pleased to find their lost camel, and they rewarded the man who had been so clever.

El camello que se perdió

José Griego y Maestas

ERAN unos mercaderes que viajaban a otro país a vender sus productos. Caminaban muy tarde, ya obscuro, se les perdió un camello. Cuando hicieron campo, vieron que faltaba uno, pero no lo pudieron encontrar.

Al otro día salieron a buscar el camello y se encontraron con un hombre que iba en dirección opuesta y le preguntaron si no había visto un camello al lado del camino. El les dijo que no lo había visto pero que les podía dar razón de él.

"¿Llevaba carga el camello?" le preguntaron ellos.

"Sí. Iba cargado y llevaba trigo del lado izquierdo," les dijo él, "y en el lado derecho llevaba miel. El camello es tuerto y le falta un diente del medio también, pero no lo he visto."

"Pues, ¿cómo si no lo has visto das la razón tan cierta de él? Tú tendrás escondido a ese camello, y quieres robártelo."

"Pues no lo he visto."

"¿Pues cómo sabes que llevaba trigo y miel?"

"Digo que llevaba trigo porque del lado izquierdo iba tirando granos de trigo, porque la carga estaría ya agujerado por los palos. Las hormiguitas estaban recogiendo los granos de trigo. Del lado derecho de la misma manera iba derramando miel y las moscas iban hechas montón por ese lado."

"Bien, ¿y cómo sabes que era tuerto?"

"Porque en la vereda que caminaba no más para el lado derecho tomaba bocados de zacate."

"¿Y cómo sabes que le faltaba un diente?"

"Porque en cada bocado que agarraba dejaba un mechoncito en medio y eso me indicaba que le faltaba un diente."

"Pues si así es" dijeron "tú eres un buen hombre y te damos albricias por la razón que nos has dado."

Fueron a buscar el camello y lo encontraron y le dieron gratificación al buen hombre que les dio tan buenas razones.

Lazy Peter and His Three-Cornered Hat

Retold by Ricardo E. Alegría

This is the story of Lazy Peter, a shameless rascal of a fellow who went from village to village making mischief.

ONE day Lazy Peter learned that a fair was being held in a certain village. He knew that a large crowd of country people would be there selling horses, cows, and other farm animals and that a large amount of money would change hands. Peter, as usual, needed money, but it was not his custom to work for it. So he set out for the village, wearing a red three-cornered hat.

The first thing he did was to stop at a stand and leave a big bag of money with the owner, asking him to keep it safely until he returned for it. Peter told the man that when he returned for the bag of money, one corner of his hat would be turned down, and that was how the owner of the stand would know him. The man promised to do this, and Peter thanked him. Then he went to the drugstore in the village and gave the druggist another bag of money, asking him to keep it until he returned with one corner of his hat turned up. The druggist agreed, and Peter left. He went to the church and asked the priest to keep another bag of money and to return it to him only when he came back with one corner of his hat twisted to the side. The priest said fine, he would do this.

Having disposed of three bags of money, Peter went to the edge of the village where the farmers were buying and selling horses and cattle. He stood and watched for a while until he decided that one of the farmers must be very rich indeed, for he had sold all of his horses and cows. Moreover, the man seemed to be a miser who was never satisfied but wanted always more and more money. This was Peter's man! He stopped beside him. It was raining; and instead of keeping his hat on to protect his head, he took it off and wrapped it carefully in his cape, as though it were very valuable. It puzzled the farmer to see Peter stand there with the rain falling on his head and his hat wrapped in his cape.

After a while he asked, "Why do you take better care of your hat than of your head?"

Peter saw that the farmer had swallowed the bait, and smiling to himself, he said that the hat was the most valuable thing in all the world and that was why he took care to protect it from the rain. The farmer's curiosity increased at this reply, and he asked Peter what was so valuable about a red three-cornered hat. Peter told him that the hat worked for him; thanks to it, he never had to work for a living because whenever he put the hat on with one of the corners turned over, people just handed him any money he asked for.

The farmer was amazed and very interested in what Peter said. As money-getting was his greatest ambition, he told Peter that he couldn't believe a word of it until he saw the hat work with his own eyes. Peter assured him that he could do this, for he, Peter, was hungry, and the hat was about to start working, since he had no money with which to buy food.

With this, Peter took out his three-cornered hat, turned one corner down, put it on his head, and told the farmer to come along and watch the hat work. Peter took the farmer to the stand. The minute the owner looked up, he handed over the bag of money Peter had left with him. The farmer stood with his mouth open in astonishment. He didn't know what to make of it. But of one thing he was sure—he had to have that hat!

Peter smiled and asked if he was satisfied, and the farmer said yes, he was. Then he asked Peter if he would sell the hat. This was just what Lazy Peter wanted, but he said no, he was not interested in selling the hat because with it, he never had to work and he always had money. The farmer said he thought that was unsound reasoning because thieves could easily steal a hat, and wouldn't it be safer to invest in a farm with cattle? So they talked, and Peter pretended to be impressed with the farmer's arguments. Finally he said yes, that he saw the point, and if the farmer would make him a good offer, he would sell the hat. The farmer, who had made up his mind to have the hat at any price, offered a thousand pesos. Peter laughed aloud and said he could make as much as that by just putting his hat on two or three times.

As they continued haggling over the price, the farmer grew more and more determined to have that hat, until, finally, he offered all he had realized from the sale of his horses and cows—ten thousand pesos in gold. Peter still pretended not to be interested, but he chuckled to himself, thinking of the trick he was about to play on the farmer. All right, he said, it was a deal. Then the farmer grew cautious and told Peter that before he handed over the ten thousand pesos, he would like to see the hat work again. Peter said that was fair enough. He put on the hat with one of the corners turned up and went with the farmer to the drugstore. The moment the druggist saw the turned-up corner, he handed over the money Peter had left with him. At this the farmer was convinced and very eager to set the hat to work for himself. He took out a bag containing ten thousand pesos in gold and was about to hand it to Peter when he had a change of heart and thought better of it. He asked Peter please to excuse him, but he had to see the hat work just once more before he could part with his gold. Peter said that that was fair enough, but now he would have to ask the farmer to give him the fine horse he was riding as well as the ten thousand pesos in gold. The farmer's interest in the hat revived, and he said it was a bargain!

Lazy Peter put on his hat again, doubled over one of the corners, and told the farmer that since he still seemed to have doubts, this time he could watch the hat work in the church. The farmer was delighted with this, his doubts were stilled, and he fairly beamed thinking of all the money he was going to make once that hat was his.

They entered the church. The priest was hearing confession, but when he saw Peter with his hat, he said, "Wait here, my son," and he went to the sacristy and returned with the bag of money Peter had left with him. Peter thanked the priest, then knelt and asked for a blessing before he left. The farmer had seen everything and was fully convinced of the hat's magic powers. As soon as they left the church, he gave Peter the ten thousand pesos in gold and told him to take the horse also. Peter tied the bag of pesos to the saddle, gave the hat to the farmer, begging him to take good care of it, spurred his horse, and galloped out of town.

As soon as he was alone, the farmer burst out laughing at the thought of the trick he had played on Lazy Peter. A hat such as this was priceless! He couldn't wait to try it. He put it on with one corner turned up and entered the butcher shop. The butcher looked at the hat, which was very handsome indeed, but said nothing. The farmer turned around, then walked up and down until the butcher asked him what he wanted. The farmer said he was waiting for the bag of money. The butcher laughed aloud and asked if he was crazy. The farmer thought that there must be something wrong with the way he had folded the hat. He took it off and doubled another corner down. But this had no effect on the butcher. So he decided to try it out some other place. He went to the mayor of the town.

The mayor, to be sure, looked at the hat but did nothing. The farmer grew desperate and decided to go to the druggist who had given Peter a bag of money. He entered and stood with the hat on. The druggist looked at him but did nothing.

The farmer became very nervous. He began to suspect that there was something very wrong. He shouted at the druggist, "Stop looking at me and hand over the bag of money!"

The druggist said he owed him nothing, and what bag of money was he talking about, anyway? As the farmer continued to shout about a bag of money and a magic hat, the druggist called the police. When they arrived, he told them that the farmer had gone out of his mind and kept demanding a bag of money. The police questioned the farmer, and he told them about the magic hat he had bought from Lazy Peter. When he heard the story, the druggist explained that Peter had left a bag of money, asking that it be returned when he appeared with a corner of his hat turned up. The owner of the stand and the priest told the same story. And I am telling you the farmer was so angry that he tore the hat to shreds and walked home.

Only Daughter

Sandra Cisneros

ONCE, several years ago, when I was just starting out my writing career, I was asked to write my own contributor's note for an anthology I was part of. I wrote: "I am the only daughter in a family of six sons. *That* explains everything."

Well, I've thought about that ever since, and yes, it explains a lot to me, but for the reader's sake I should have written: "I am the only daughter in a *Mexican* family of six sons." Or even "I am the only daughter of a Mexican farmer and a Mexican-American mother." Or: "I am the only daughter of a working-class family of nine." All of these had everything to do with who I am today.

I was/am the only daughter and *only* a daughter. Being an only daughter in a family of six sons forced me by circumstance to spend a lot of time by myself because my brothers felt it beneath them to play with a *girl* in public. But that aloneness, that loneliness, was good for a would-be writer—it allowed me time to think and think, to imagine, to read and prepare myself.

Being only a daughter for my father meant my destiny would lead me to become someone's wife. That's what he believed. But when I was in the fifth grade and shared my plans for college with him, I was sure he understood. I remember my father saying, "*Que bueno, mi'ja,* that's good." That meant a lot to me, especially since my brothers thought the idea hilarious. What I didn't realize was that my father thought college was good for girls—good for finding a husband. After four years in college and two more in graduate school and still no husband, my father shakes his head even now and says I wasted all that education.

In retrospect, I'm lucky my father believed daughters were meant for husbands. It meant it didn't matter if I majored in something silly like English. After all, I'd find a nice professional eventually, right? This allowed me the liberty to putter about embroidering my little poems and stories without my father interrupting with so much as a "What's that you're writing?"

But the truth is, I wanted him to interrupt. I wanted my father to understand what it was I was scribbling, to introduce me as "My only daughter, the writer." Not as "This is only my daughter. She teaches." *El maestra*—teacher. Not ever *profesora.*

In a sense, everything I have ever written has been for him, to win his approval even though I know my father can't read English words, even though my father's only reading includes the brown-ink *Esto* sports magazines from Mexico City and the bloody *¡Alarma!* magazines that feature yet another sighting of *La Virgen de Guadalupe* on a tortilla or a wife's revenge on her philandering husband by bashing his skull in with a *molcajete* (a kitchen mortar made of volcanic rock). Or the *fotonovelas,* the little picture paperbacks with tragedy and trauma erupting from the characters' mouths in bubbles.

My father represents, then, the public majority. A public who is disinterested in reading, and yet one whom I am writing about and for and privately trying to woo.

When we were growing up in Chicago, we moved a lot because of my father. He suffered bouts of nostalgia. Then we'd have to let go our flat, store the furniture with mother's relatives, load the station wagon with baggage and bologna sandwiches, and head south. To Mexico City.

We came back, of course. To yet another Chicago flat, another Chicago neighborhood, another Catholic school. Each time, my father would seek out the parish priest in order to get a tuition break and complain or boast: "I have seven sons."

He meant *siete hijos,* seven children, but he translated it as "sons." "I have seven sons." To anyone who would listen. The Sears Roebuck employee who sold us the washing machine. The short-order cook where my father ate his ham-and-eggs breakfasts. "I have seven sons." As if he deserved a medal from the state.

My papa. He didn't mean anything by that mistranslation, I'm sure. But somehow I could feel myself being erased. I'd tug my father's sleeve and whisper: "Not seven sons. Six! and *one daughter.*"

When my oldest brother graduated from medical school, he fulfilled my father's dream that we study hard and use this—our heads, instead of this—our hands. Even now my father's hands are thick and yellow, stubbed by a history of hammer and nails and twine and coils and springs. "Use this," my father said, tapping his head, "and not this," showing us those hands. He always looked tired when he said it.

Wasn't college an investment? And hadn't I spent all those years in college? And if I didn't marry, what was it all for? Why would anyone go to college and then choose to be poor? Especially someone who had always been poor.

Last year, after ten years of writing professionally, the financial rewards started to trickle in. My second National Endowment for the Arts Fellowship. A guest professorship at the University of California, Berkeley. My book, which sold to a major New York publishing house.

At Christmas, I flew home to Chicago. The house was throbbing, same as always; hot *tamales* and sweet *tamales* hissing in my mother's pressure cooker, and everybody—my mother, six brothers, wives, babies, aunts, cousins—talking too loud and at the same time, like in a Fellini film, because that's just how we are.

I went upstairs to my father's room. One of my stories had just been translated into Spanish and published in an anthology of Chicano writing, and I wanted to show it to him. Ever since he recovered from a stroke two years ago, my father likes to spend his leisure hours horizontally. And that's how I found him, watching a Pedro Infante movie on Galavision and eating rice pudding.

There was a glass filmed with milk on the bedside table. There were several vials of pills and balled Kleenex. And on the floor, one black sock and a plastic urinal that I didn't want to look at but looked at anyway. Pedro Infante was about to burst into song, and my father was laughing.

I'm not sure if it was because my story was translated into Spanish or because it was published in Mexico or perhaps because the story dealt with Tepeyac, the *colonia* my father was raised in and the house he grew up in, but at any rate, my father punched the mute button on his remote control and read my story.

I sat on the bed next to my father and waited. He read it very slowly. As if he were reading each line over and over. He laughed at all the right places and read lines he liked out loud. He pointed and asked questions: "Is this So-and-so?"

"Yes," I said. He kept reading.

When he was finally finished, after what seemed like hours, my father looked up and asked: "Where can we get more copies of this for the relatives?"

Of all the wonderful things that happened to me last year, that was the most wonderful.

A Shot at It

from

When I Was Puerto Rican

Esmeralda Santiago

Te conozco bacalao, aunque vengas disfrazao.
I recognize you salted codfish, even if you're in disguise.

WHILE Francisco was still alive, we had moved to Ellery Street.
That meant I had to change schools, so Mami walked me to P.S.
33, where I would attend ninth grade. The first week I was there
I was given a series of tests that showed that even though I
couldn't speak English very well, I read and wrote it at the tenth-
grade level. So they put me in 9-3, with the smart kids.

One morning, Mr. Barone, a guidance counsellor, called me to
his office. He was short, with a big head and large hazel eyes under
shapely eyebrows. His nose was long and round at the tip. He
dressed in browns and yellows and often perched his tortoiseshell
glasses on his forehead, as if he had another set of eyes up there.

"So," he pushed his glasses up, "what do you want to be when
you grow up?"

"I don't know."

He shuffled through some papers. "Let's see here . . . you're
fourteen, is that right?"

"Yes, sir."

"And you've never thought about what you want to be?"

When I was very young, I wanted to be a *jíbara*. When I was
older, I wanted to be a cartographer, then a topographer. But since
we'd come to Brooklyn, I'd not thought about the future much.

"No, sir."

He pulled his glasses down to where they belonged and shuffled through the papers again.

"Do you have any hobbies?" I didn't know what he meant.
"Hobbies, hobbies," he flailed his hands, as if he were juggling,
"things you like to do after school."

"Ah, yes." I tried to imagine what I did at home that might
qualify as a hobby. "I like to read."

He seemed disappointed. "Yes, we know that about you." He pulled out a paper and stared at it. "One of the tests we gave you was an aptitude test. It tells us what kinds of things you might be good at. The tests show that you would be good at helping people. Do you like to help people?"

I was afraid to contradict tests. "Yes, sir."

"There's a high school we can send you where you can study biology and chemistry which will prepare you for a career in nursing."

I screwed up my face. He consulted the papers again.

"You would also do well in communications. Teaching maybe."

I remembered Miss Brown standing in front of a classroom full of rowdy teenagers, some of them taller than she was.

"I don't like to teach."

Mr. Barone pushed his glasses up again and leaned over the stack of papers on his desk. "Why don't you think about it and get back to me," he said, closing the folder with my name across the top. He put his hand flat on it, as if squeezing something out. "You're a smart girl, Esmeralda. Let's try to get you into an academic school so that you have a shot at college."

On the way home, I walked with another new ninth grader, Yolanda. She had been in New York for three years but knew as little English as I did. We spoke in Spanglish, a combination of English and Spanish in which we hopped from one language to the other depending on which word came first.

"*Te preguntó el* Mr. Barone, you know, *lo que querías hacer* when you grow up?" I asked.

"*Sí, pero,* I didn't know. *¿Y tú?*"

"*Yo tampoco.* He said, *que* I like to help people. *Pero,* you know, *a mí no me gusta mucho la gente.*" When she heard me say I didn't like people much, Yolanda looked at me from the corner of her eye, waiting to become the exception.

By the time I said it, she had dashed up the stairs of her building. She didn't wave as she ducked in, and the next day she wasn't friendly. I walked around the rest of the day in embarrassed isolation, knowing that somehow I have given myself away to the only friend I'd made at Junior High School 33. I had to either take back my words or live with the consequences of stating what was becoming the truth. I'd never said that to anyone, not even to myself. It was an added weight, but I wasn't about to trade it for companionship.

A few days later, Mr. Barone called me back to his office.

"Well?" Tiny green flecks burned around the black pupils of his hazel eyes.

The night before, Mami had called us into the living room. On the television "fifty of America's most beautiful girls" paraded in ruffled tulle dresses before a tinsel waterfall.

"Aren't they lovely?" Mami murmured, as the girls, escorted by boys in uniform, floated by the camera, twirled, and disappeared behind a screen to the strains of a waltz and an announcer's dramatic voice calling their names, ages, and states. Mami sat mesmerized through the whole pageant.

"I'd like to become a model," I said to Mr. Barone.

He stared at me, pulled his glasses down from his forehead, looked at the papers inside the folder with my name on it, and glared. "A model?" His voice was gruff, as if he were more comfortable yelling at people than talking to them.

"I want to be on television."

"Oh, then you want to be an actress," in a tone that said this was only a slight improvement over my first career choice. We stared at one another for a few seconds. He pushed his glasses up to his forehead again and reached for a book on the shelf in back of him. "I only know of one school that trains actresses, but we've never sent them a student from here."

Performing Arts, the write-up said, was an academic, as opposed to a vocational, public school that trained students wishing to pursue a career in theater, music, and dance.

"It says here that you have to audition." He stood up and held the book closer to the faint gray light coming through the narrow window high on his wall. "Have you ever performed in front of an audience?"

"I was announcer in my school show in Puerto Rico," I said. "And I recite poetry. There, not here."

He closed the book and held it against his chest. His right index finger thumped a rhythm on his lower lip. "Let me call them and find out exactly what you need to do. Then we can talk some more."

I left his office strangely happy, confident that something good had just happened, not knowing exactly what.

"I'm not afraid . . . I'm not afraid . . . I'm not afraid." Every day I walked home from school repeating those words. The broad streets and sidewalks that had impressed me so on the first day we had arrived had become as familiar as the dirt road from Macún to the highway. Only my curiosity about the people who lived behind these walls ended where the façades of the buildings opened into dark hallways or locked doors. Nothing good, I imagined, could be happening inside if so many locks had to be breached to go in or step out.

It was on these tense walks home from school that I decided I had to get out of Brooklyn. Mami had chosen this as our home, and just like every other time we'd moved, I'd had to go along with her because I was a child who had no choice. But I wasn't willing to go along with her on this one.

"How can people live like this?" I shrieked once, desperate to run across a field, to feel grass under my feet instead of pavement.

"Like what?" Mami asked, looking around our apartment, the kitchen and living room crisscrossed with sagging lines of drying diapers and bedclothes.

"Everyone on top of each other. No room to do anything. No air."

"Do you want to go back to Macún, to live like savages, with no electricity, no toilets . . ."

"At least you could step outside every day without somebody trying to kill you."

"Ay, Negi, stop exaggerating!"

"I hate my life!" I yelled.

"Then do something about it," she yelled back.

Until Mr. Barone showed me the listing for Performing Arts High School, I hadn't known what to do.

"The auditions are in less than a month. You have to learn a monologue, which you will perform in front of a panel. If you do well, and your grades here are good, you might get into the school."

Mr. Barone took charge of preparing me for my audition to Performing Arts. He selected a speech from *The Silver Cord*, a play by Sidney Howard, first performed in 1926, but whose action took place in a New York drawing room circa 1905.

"Mr. Gatti, the English teacher," he said, "will coach you. . . . And Mrs. Johnson will talk to you about what to wear and things like that."

I was to play Christina, a young married woman confronting her mother-in-law. I learned the monologue phonetically from Mr. Gatti. It opened with "You belong to a type that's very common in this country, Mrs. Phelps—a type of self-centered, self-pitying, son-devouring tigress, with unmentionable proclivities suppressed on the side."

"We don't have time to study the meaning of every word," Mr. Gatti said. "Just make sure you pronounce every word correctly."

Mrs. Johnson, who taught Home Economics, called me to her office.

"Is that how you enter a room?" she asked the minute I came in. "Try again, only this time, don't barge in. Step in slowly, head up, back straight, a nice smile on your face. That's it." I took a deep breath and waited. "Now sit. No, not like that. Don't just plop down. Float down to the chair with your knees together." She demonstrated, and I copied her. "That's better. What do you do with your hands? No, don't hold your chin like that; it's not lady-like. Put your hands on your lap, and leave them there. Don't use them so much when you talk."

I sat stiff as a cutout while Mrs. Johnson and Mr. Barone asked me questions they thought the panel at Performing Arts would ask.

"Where are you from?"

"Puerto Rico."

"No," Mrs. Johnson said, "Porto Rico. Keep your *r*'s soft. Try again."

"Do you have any hobbies?" Mr. Barone asked. Now I knew what to answer.

"I enjoy dancing and the movies."

"Why do you want to come to this school?"

Mrs. Johnson and Mr. Barone had worked on my answer if this question should come up.

"I would like to study at Performing Arts because of its academic program and so that I may be trained as an actress."

"Very good, very good!" Mr. Barone rubbed his hands together, twinkled his eyes at Mrs. Johnson. "I think we have a shot at this."

"Remember," Mrs. Johnson said, "when you shop for your audition dress, look for something very simple in dark colors."

Mami bought me a red plaid wool jumper with a crisp white shirt, my first pair of stockings, and penny loafers. The night before, she rolled up my hair in pink curlers that cut into my scalp and made it hard to sleep. For the occasion, I was allowed to wear eye makeup and a little lipstick.

"You look so grown up!" Mami said, her voice sad but happy, as I twirled in front of her and Tata.

"Toda una señorita," Tata said, her eyes misty.

We set out for the audition on an overcast January morning heavy with the threat of snow.

"Why couldn't you choose a school close to home?" Mami grumbled as we got on the train to Manhattan. I worried that even if I were accepted, she wouldn't let me go because it was so far from home, one hour each way by subway. But in spite of her complaints, she was proud that I was good enough to be considered for such a famous school. And she actually seemed excited that I would be leaving the neighborhood.

"You'll be exposed to a different class of people," she assured me, and I felt the force of her ambition without knowing exactly what she meant.

Three women sat behind a long table in a classroom where the desks and chairs had been pushed against a wall. As I entered I held my head up and smiled, and then I floated down to the chair in front of them, clasped my hands on my lap, and smiled some more.

"Good morning," said the tall one with hair the color of sand. She was big boned and solid, with intense blue eyes, a generous mouth, and soothing hands with short fingernails. She was dressed in shades of beige from head to toe and wore no makeup and no jewelry except for the gold chain that held her glasses just above her full bosom. Her voice was rich, modulated, each word pronounced as if she were inventing it.

Next to her sat a very small woman with very high heels. Her cropped hair was pouffed around her face, with bangs brushing the tips of her long false lashes, her huge dark brown eyes were thickly lined in black all around, and her small mouth was carefully drawn in and painted cerise. Her suntanned face turned toward me with the innocent curiosity of a lively baby. She was dressed in black, with many gold chains around her neck, big earrings, several bracelets, and large stone rings on the fingers of both hands.

The third woman was tall, small boned, thin, but shapely. Her dark hair was pulled flat against her skull into a knot in back of her head. Her face was all angles and light, with fawn-like dark brown eyes, a straight nose, full lips painted just a shade pinker than their natural color. Silky forest green cuffs peeked out from the sleeves of her burgundy suit. Diamond studs winked from perfect earlobes.

I had dreamed of this moment for several weeks. More than anything, I wanted to impress the panel with my talent, so that I would be accepted into Performing Arts and leave Brooklyn every day. And, I hoped, one day I would never go back.

But the moment I faced these three impeccably groomed women, I forgot my English and Mrs. Johnson's lessons on how to behave like a lady. In the agony of trying to answer their barely comprehensible questions, I jabbed my hands here and there, forming words with my fingers because the words refused to leave my mouth.

"Why don't you let us hear your monologue now?" the woman with the dangling glasses asked softly.

I stood up abruptly, and my chair clattered onto its side two feet from where I stood. I picked it up, wishing with all my strength that a thunderbolt would strike me dead to ashes on the spot.

"It's all right," she said. "Take a breath. We know you're nervous."

I closed my eyes and breathed deeply, walked to the middle of the room, and began my monologue.

"Ju bee lonh 2 a type dats berry cómo is dis kuntree, Meessees Felps. A type off selfcent red self pee tee in sun de boring tie gress wid on men shon ah ball pro klee bee tees on de side."

In spite of Mr. Gatti's reminders that I should speak slowly and enunciate every word, even if I didn't understand it, I recited my three-minute monologue in one minute flat.

The small woman's long lashes seemed to have grown with amazement. The elegant woman's serene face twitched with controlled laughter. The tall one dressed in beige smiled sweetly.

"Thank you, dear," she said. "Could you wait outside for a few moments?"

I resisted the urge to curtsy. The long hallway had narrow wainscotting halfway up to the high ceiling. Single bulb lamps hung from long cords, creating yellow puddles of light on the polished brown linoleum tile. A couple of girls my age sat on straight chairs next to their mothers, waiting their turn. They looked up as I came out and the door shut behind me. Mami stood up from her chair at the end of the hall. She looked as scared as I felt.

"What happened?"

"Nothing," I mumbled, afraid that if I began telling her about it, I would break into tears in front of the other people, whose eyes followed me and Mami as we walked to the EXIT sign. "I have to wait here a minute."

"Did they say anything?"

"No, I'm just supposed to wait."

We leaned against the wall. Across from us there was a bulletin board with newspaper clippings about former students. On the ragged edge, a neat person had printed in blue ink, "P.A." and the year the actor, dancer, or musician had graduated. I closed my eyes and tried to picture myself on that bulletin board, with "P.A. '66" across the top.

The door at the end of the hall opened, and the woman in beige poked her head out.

"Esmeralda?"

"Sí, I mean, here." I raised my hand.

She led me into the room. There was another girl in there, whom she introduced as Bonnie, a junior at the school.

"Do you know what a pantomime is?" the woman asked. I nodded. "You and Bonnie are sisters decorating a Christmas tree."

Bonnie looked a lot like Juanita Marín, whom I had last seen in Macún four years earlier. We decided where the invisible Christmas tree would be, and we sat on the floor and pretended we were taking decorations out of boxes and hanging them on the branches.

My family had never had a Christmas tree, but I remembered how once I had helped Papi wind colored lights around the eggplant bush that divided our land from Doña Ana's. We started at the bottom and wound the wire with tiny red bulbs around and around until we ran out; then Papi plugged another cord to it and we kept going until the branches hung heavy with light and the bush looked like it was on fire.

Before long I had forgotten where I was, and that the tree didn't exist and Bonnie was not my sister. She pretended to hand me a very delicate ball, and just before I took it, she made like it fell to the ground and shattered. I was petrified that Mami would come in and yell at us for breaking her favorite decoration. Just as I began to pick up the tiny fragments of nonexistent crystal, a voice broke in. "Thank you."

Bonnie got up, smiled, and went out.

The elegant woman stretched her hand out for me to shake. "We will notify your school in a few weeks. It was very nice to meet you."

I shook hands all around then backed out of the room in a fog, silent, as if the pantomime had taken my voice and the urge to speak.

On the way home Mami kept asking what had happened, and I kept mumbling, "Nothing. Nothing happened," ashamed that, after all the hours of practice with Mrs. Johnson, Mr. Barone, and Mr. Gatti, after the expense of new clothes and shoes, after Mami had to take a day off from work to take me into Manhattan, after all that, I had failed the audition and would never, ever, get out of Brooklyn.

> *El mismo jíbaro con diferente caballo.*
> *Same jíbaro, different horse.*

A DECADE after my graduation from Performing Arts, I visited the school. I was by then living in Boston, a scholarship student at Harvard University. The tall, elegant woman of my audition had become my mentor through my three years there. Since my graduation, she had married the school principal.

"I remember your audition," she said, her chiseled face dreamy, her lips toying with a smile that she seemed, still, to have to control.

I had forgotten the skinny brown girl with the curled hair, wool jumper, and lively hands. But she hadn't. She told me that the panel had had to ask me to leave so that they could laugh, because it was so funny to see a fourteen-year-old Puerto Rican girl jabbering out a monologue about a possessive mother-in-law at the turn of the century, the words incomprehensible because they went by so fast.

"We admired," she said, "the courage it took to stand in front of us and do what you did."

"So you mean I didn't get into the school because of my talent, but because I had chutzpah?" We both laughed.

"Are any of your sisters and brothers in college?"

"No, I'm the only one, so far."

"How many of you are there?"

"By the time I graduated from high school there were eleven of us."

"Eleven!" She looked at me for a long time, until I had to look down. "Do you ever think about how far you've come?" she asked.

"No." I answered. "I never stop to think about it. It might jinx the momentum."

"Let me tell you another story, then," she said. "The first day of your first year, you were absent. We called your house. You said you couldn't come to school because you had nothing to wear. I wasn't sure if you were joking. I asked to speak to your mother, and you translated what she said. She needed you to go somewhere with her to interpret. At first you wouldn't tell me where, but then you admitted you were going to the welfare office. You were crying, and I had to assure you that you were not the only student in this school whose family received public assistance. The next day you were here, bright and eager. And now here you are, about to graduate from Harvard."

"I'm glad you made that phone call," I said.

"And I'm glad you came to see me, but right now I have to teach a class." She stood up, as graceful as I remembered. "Take care."

Her warm embrace, fragrant of expensive perfume, took me by surprise. "Thank you," I said as she went around the corner to her classroom.

I walked the halls of the school, looking for the room where my life had changed. It was across from the science lab, a few doors down from the big bulletin board where someone with neat handwriting still wrote the letters "P.A." followed by the graduating year along the edges of newspaper clippings featuring famous alumni.

"P.A. '66," I said to no one in particular. "One of these days."

Lessons of Love
from Silent Dancing

Judith Ortiz Cofer

I FELL in love, or my hormones awakened from their long slumber in my body, and suddenly the goal of my days was focused on one thing: to catch a glimpse of my secret love. And it had to remain secret, because I had, of course, in the great tradition of tragic romance, chosen to love a boy who was totally out of my reach. He was not Puerto Rican; he was Italian and rich. He was also an older man. He was a senior at the high school when I came in as a freshman. I first saw him in the hall, leaning casually on a wall that was the border line between girl-side and boyside for underclassmen. He looked extraordinarily like a young Marlon Brando—down to the ironic little smile. The total of what I knew about the boy who starred in every one of my awkward fantasies was this: that he was the nephew of the man who owned the supermarket on my block; that he often had parties at his parents' beautiful home in the suburbs, which I would hear about; that this family had money (which came to our school in many ways); and that—this fact made my knees weak—he worked at the store near my apartment building on weekends and in the summer.

My mother could not understand why I became so eager to be the one sent out on her endless errands. I pounced on every opportunity from Friday to late Saturday afternoon to go after eggs, cigarettes, milk (I tried to drink as much of it as possible, although I hated the stuff)—the staple items that she would order from the "American" store.

Week after week I wandered up and down the aisles, taking furtive glances at the stock room in the back, breathlessly hoping to see my prince. Not that I had a plan. I felt like a pilgrim waiting for a glimpse of Mecca. I did not expect him to notice me. It was sweet agony.

One day I did see him. Dressed in a white outfit, like a surgeon: white pants and shirt, white cap, and (gross sight, but not to my love-glazed eyes) blood-smeared butcher's apron. He was helping to drag a side of beef into the freezer storage area of the store. I must have stood there like an idiot, because I remember that he did see me; he even spoke to me! I could have died. I think he said, "Excuse me," and smiled vaguely in my direction.

After that, I *willed* occasions to go to the supermarket. I watched my mother's pack of cigarettes empty ever so slowly. I wanted her to smoke them fast. I drank milk and forced it on my brother (although a second glass for him had to be bought with my share of Fig Newton cookies, which we both liked, but we were restricted to one row each). I gave my cookies up for love, and watched my mother smoke her L&M's with so little enthusiasm that I thought that she might be cutting down on her smoking or maybe even giving up the habit. At this crucial time!

I thought I had kept my lonely romance a secret. Often I cried hot tears on my pillow for the things that kept us apart. In my mind there was no doubt that he would never notice me (and that is why I felt free to stare at him—I was invisible). He could not see me because I was a skinny Puerto Rican girl, a freshman who did not belong to any group he associated with.

At the end of the year I found out that I had not been invisible. I learned one little lesson about human nature—adulation leaves a scent, one that we are all equipped to recognize, and no matter how insignificant the source, we seek it.

In June the nuns at our school would always arrange for some cultural extravaganza. In my freshman year it was a Roman banquet. We had been studying Greek drama (as a prelude to Church history—it was at a fast clip that we galloped through Sophocles and Euripides toward the early Christian martyrs), and our young, energetic Sister Agnes was in the mood for spectacle. She ordered the entire student body (it was a small group of under three hundred students) to have our mothers make us togas out of sheets. She handed out a pattern on mimeo pages fresh out of the machine. I remember the intense smell of the alcohol on the sheets of paper and how almost everyone in the auditorium brought theirs to their noses and inhaled deeply—mimeographed handouts were the school-day buzz that the new Xerox generation of kids is missing out on. Then, as the last couple of weeks of school dragged on, the city of Paterson becoming a concrete oven and us wilting in our uncomfortable uniforms, we labored like frantic Roman slaves to build a splendid banquet hall in our small auditorium. Sister Agnes wanted a raised dais where the host and hostess would be regally enthroned.

She had already chosen our Senator and Lady from among our

ranks. The Lady was to be a beautiful new student named Sophia, a recent Polish immigrant, whose English was still practically unintelligible, but whose features, classically perfect without a trace of makeup, enthralled us. Everyone talked about her gold hair cascading her waist, and her voice, which could carry a note right up to heaven in choir. The nuns wanted her for God. They kept saying that she had a vocation. We just looked at her in awe, and the boys seemed afraid of her. She just smiled and did as she was told. I don't know what she thought of it all. The main privilege of beauty is that others will do almost everything for you, including thinking.

Her partner was to be our best basketball player, a tall, red-haired senior whose family sent its many offspring to our school. Together, Sophia and her Senator looked like the best combination of immigrant genes our community could produce. It did not occur to me to ask then whether anything but their physical beauty qualified them for the starring roles in our production. I had the highest average in the Church history class, but I was given the part of one of many "Roman citizens." I was to sit in front of the plastic fruit and recite a greeting in Latin along with the rest of the school when our hosts came into the hall and took their places on their throne.

On the night of our banquet, my father escorted me in my toga to the door of our school. I felt foolish in my awkwardly draped sheet (blouse and skirt required underneath). My mother had no great skill as a seamstress. The best she could do was hem a skirt or a pair of pants. That night I would have traded her for a peasant woman with a golden needle. I saw other Roman ladies emerging from their parents' cars looking authentic in sheets of material that folded over their bodies like the garments on a statue by Michelangelo. How did they do it? How was it that I always got it just slightly wrong, and worse, I believed that other people were just too polite to mention it. "The poor little Puerto Rican girl," I could hear them thinking. But in reality, I must have been my worst critic, self-conscious as I was.

Soon, we were all sitting at our circle of tables joined together around the dais. Sophia glittered like a golden statue. Her smile was beatific: a perfect, silent Roman lady. Her Senator looked uncomfortable, glancing around at his buddies, perhaps waiting for the ridicule that he would surely get in the locker room later. The nuns in their black habits stood in the background watching us. What were they supposed to be, the Fates? Nubian slaves? The dancing girls did their modest little dance to tinny music from their finger cymbals; then the speeches were made. Then the grape juice "wine" was raised in a toast to the Roman Empire we all knew would fall within the week—before finals, anyway.

All during the program I had been in a state of controlled hysteria. My secret love sat across the room from me looking supremely bored. I watched his every move, taking him in gluttonously. I relished the shadow of his eyelashes on his ruddy cheeks, his pouty lips smirking sarcastically at the ridiculous sight of our little play. Once he slumped down on his chair, and our sergeant-at-arms nun came over and tapped him sharply on his shoulder. He drew himself up slowly, with disdain. I loved his rebellious spirit. I believed myself still invisible to him in my "nothing" status as I looked upon my beloved. But toward the end of the evening, as we stood chanting our farewells in Latin, he looked straight across the room and into my eyes! How did I survive the killing power of those dark pupils? I trembled in a new way. I was not cold—I was burning! Yet I shook from the inside out, feeling lightheaded, dizzy.

The room began to empty and I headed for the girls' lavatory. I wanted to relish the miracle in silence. I did not think for a minute that anything more would follow. I was satisfied with the enormous favor of a look from my beloved. I took my time, knowing that my father would be waiting outside for me, impatient, perhaps glowing in the dark in his phosphorescent white Navy uniform. The others would ride home. I would walk home with my father, both of us in costume. I wanted as few witnesses as possible. When I could no longer hear the crowds in the hallway, I emerged from the bathroom, still under the spell of those mesmerizing eyes.

The lights had been turned off in the hallway, and all I could see was the lighted stairwell, at the bottom of which a nun would be stationed. My father would be waiting just outside. I nearly screamed when I felt someone grab me by the waist. But my mouth was quickly covered by someone else's mouth. I was being kissed. My first kiss and I could not even tell who it was. I pulled away to see that face not two inches away from mine. It was he. He smiled down at me. Did I have a silly expression on my face? My glasses felt crooked on my nose. I was unable to move or to speak. More gently, he lifted my chin and touched his lips to mine. This time I did not forget to enjoy it. Then, like the phantom lover that he was, he walked away into the darkened corridor and disappeared.

I don't know how long I stood there. My body was changing right there in the hallway of a Catholic school. My cells were tuning up like musicians in an orchestra, and my heart was a chorus. It was an opera I was composing, and I wanted to stand very still and just listen. But of course, I heard my father's voice talking to the nun. I was in trouble if he had had to ask about me. I hurried down the stairs, making up a story on the way about feeling sick. That would explain my flushed face and it would buy me a little privacy when I got home.

The next day Father announced at the breakfast table that he was leaving on a six-month tour of Europe with the Navy in a few weeks and that at the end of the school year my mother, my brother, and I would be sent to Puerto Rico to stay for half a year at Mamá's (my mother's mother) house. I was devastated. This was the usual routine for us. We had always gone to Mamá's to stay when Father was away for long periods. But this year it was different for me. I was in love, and . . . my heart knocked against my bony chest at this thought . . . he loved me too? I broke into sobs and left the table.

In the next week I discovered the inexorable truth about parents. They can actually carry on with their plans right through tears, threats, and the awful spectacle of a teenager's broken heart. My father left me to my mother, who impassively packed while I explained over and over that I was at a crucial time in my studies and that if I left my entire life would be ruined. All she would say was, "You are an intelligent girl, you'll catch up." Her head was filled with visions of casa and family reunions, long gossip sessions with her mamá and sisters. What did she care that I was losing my one chance at true love?

In the meantime I tried desperately to see him. I thought he would look for me too. But the few times I saw him in the hallway, he was always rushing away. It would be long weeks of confusion and pain before I realized that the kiss was nothing but a little trophy for his ego. He had no interest in me other than as his adorer. He was flattered by my silent worship of him, and he had *bestowed* a kiss on me to please himself and to fan the flames. I learned a lesson about the battle of the sexes then that I have never forgotten: The object is not always to win, but most times simply to keep your opponent (synonymous at times with "the loved one") guessing.

But this is too cynical a view to sustain in the face of that overwhelming rush of emotion that is first love. And in thinking back about my own experience with it, I can be objective only to the point where I recall how sweet the anguish was, how caught up in the moment I felt, and how every nerve in my body was involved in this salute to life. Later, much later, after what seemed like an eternity of dragging the weight of unrequited love around with me, I learned to make myself visible and to relish the little battles required to win the greatest prize of all. And much later, I read and understood Camus's statement about the subject that concerns both adolescent and philosopher alike: If love were easy, life would be too simple.

The Talk

Gary Soto

MY best friend and I knew that we were going to grow up to be ugly. On a backyard lawn—the summer light falling west of the mulberry tree where the house of the most beautiful girl on our street stood—we talked about what we could do: shake the second-base dirt from our hair, wash our hands of frog smells and canal water, and learn to smile without showing our crooked teeth. We had to stop spitting when girls were looking and learn not to pile food onto a fork and into a fat cheek already churning hot grub.

We were twelve, with lean bodies that were beginning to grow in weird ways. First, our heads got large, but our necks wavered, frail as crisp tulips. The eyes stayed small as well, receding into pencil dots on each side of an unshapely nose that cast remarkable shadows when we turned sideways. It seemed that Scott's legs sprouted muscle and renegade veins, but his arms, blue with ink markings, stayed short and hung just below his waist. My gangly arms nearly touched my kneecaps. In this way, I was built for picking up grounders and doing cartwheels, my arms swaying just inches from the summery grass.

We sat on the lawn, with the porch light off, waiting for the beautiful girl to turn on her bedroom light and read on her stomach with one leg stirring the air. This stirred us, and our dream was a clean dream of holding hands and airing out our loneliness by walking up and down the block.

When Scott asked whom I was going to marry, I said a brown girl from the valley. He said that he was going to marry a strawberry blonde who would enjoy Millerton Lake, dirty as it was. I said mine would like cats and the sea and would think nothing of getting up at night from a warm, restless bed and sitting in the yard under the icy stars. Scott said his wife would work for the first year or so, because he would go to trade school in refrigeration. Since our town was made with what was left over after God made hell, there was money in air conditioning, he reasoned.

I said that while my wife would clean the house and stir pots of nice grub, I would drive a truck to my job as a carpenter, which would allow me to use my long arms. I would need only a stepladder to hand a fellow worker on the roof a pinch of nails. I could hammer, saw, lift beams into place, and see the work I got done at the end of the day. Of course, she might like to work, and that would be okay, because then we could buy two cars and wave at each other if we should see the other drive by. In the evenings, we would drink Kool-Aid and throw a slipper at our feisty dog at least a hundred times before we went inside for a Pop-Tart and hot chocolate.

Scott said he would work hard too, but now and then he would find money on the street and the two of them could buy extra things like a second TV for the bedroom and a Doughboy swimming pool for his three kids. He planned on having three kids and a ranch house on the river, where he could dip a hand in the water, drink, and say, "Ahh, tastes good."

But that would be years later. Now we had to do something about our looks. We plucked at the grass and flung it into each other's faces.

"Rotten luck," Scott said. "My arms are too short. Look at 'em."

"Maybe we can lift weights. This would make up for our looks," I said.

"I don't think so," Scott said, depressed. "People like people with nice faces."

He was probably right. I turned onto my stomach, a stalk of grass in my mouth. "Even if I'm ugly, my wife's going to be good-looking," I said. "She'll have a lot of dresses and I'll have more shirts than I have now. Do you know how much carpenters make?"

Then I saw the bedroom light come on and the beautiful girl walk into the room drying her hair with a towel. I nudged Scott's short arm and he saw what I saw. We flicked the stalks of grass, stood up, and walked over to the fence to look at her scrub her hair dry. She plopped onto the bed and began to comb it, slowly at first because it was tangled. With a rubber band, she tied it back, and picked up a book that was thick as a good-sized sandwich.

Scott and I watched her read a book, now both legs in the air and twined together, her painted toenails like red petals. She turned the pages slowly, very carefully, and now and then lowered her face into the pillow. She looked sad but beautiful, and we didn't know what to do except nudge each other in the heart and creep away to the front yard.

"I can't stand it anymore. We have to talk about this," Scott said.

"If I try, I think I can make myself better looking," I said. "I read an article about a girl whitening her teeth with water and flour."

So we walked up the street, depressed. For every step I took, Scott took two, his short arms pumping to keep up. For every time Scott said, "I think we're ugly," I said two times, "Yeah, yeah, we're in big trouble."

Why Fear Spanish?

Carlos Alberto Montaner

I WAS walking quietly with my wife on a sidewalk in Miami Beach. We were speaking Spanish, of course, because that is our language. Suddenly, we were accosted by a spry little old lady, wearing a baseball cap and sneakers, who told us: "Talk English. You are in the United States." She continued on her way at once, without stopping to see our reaction. The expression on her face, curiously, was not that of somebody performing a rude action, but of somebody performing a sacred patriotic duty.

And the truth is that the lady in question was not an eccentric madwoman. Thousands, millions of monolingual Americans are mortified that in their country there is a vast minority that constantly speaks a language that they do not understand. It disturbs them to hear Spanish prattle in shops, at work, in restaurants. They are irritated when conversations they do not understand are held in their presence. Indeed, they are upset to stumble across Spanish-language stations on their radio or television dial, or by the fact that the *Miami Herald* occasionally includes an unsolicited supplement in the language of Castile.

Actually, the old lady's attitude was natural. Miami Beach is, more or less, the United States. And the language of the United States is English. Moreover, one of the key elements in the configuration of a nation is its language. A monolingual American who suddenly finds himself on Miami's Calle Ocho or in San Francisco's Chinatown has the feeling that he is not in his own country. And when one is not in one's own country, one feels endangered. Not faced with any danger in particular, but subject to that diffuse and irrational fear caused by words, expressions, and traits different from our own.

Hostility to a foreign language on our own turf generally does not come from balanced reflection on the advantages or disadvantages of linguistic homogeneity, but from an atavistic reaction that probably has been part of human nature for millions of years, when the differences between the groups that populated the planet might result in the death or destruction of the other. Much more recently, as far as the Greeks were concerned, barbarity flowed from ignorance of Greek. Since then—and, I fear, for all time—foreigners are inevitably considered barbarians.

All right; thus far, I have confined myself to a kindly comprehension of prejudice, but there are other factors that cannot be ignored in approaching this unhappy problem. A language is much more than a way to communicate. By one's own language—and on this Edward Sapir wrote much and well—one masters reality, one takes to oneself and understands all that exists. All: history, interpersonal relations, the most intimate and definitive emotions. For example, anybody who learns to love in one language will never be able spontaneously to translate his expressions of affection into a language acquired later.

We quarrel, are jealous, love, and hate with certain words, with certain tones, with certain inflections of the voice learned in childhood and adapted to a given set of gestures that also cannot be transported into another language. And this matching of word and message comes solely in the mother tongue. "Language," said the Spanish writer Miguel Unamuno, "is the blood of the spirit." He was right. We cannot do without our own tongue without brutally mutilating our individual consciousness, without being left without blood.

If this is so, is it reasonable to ask millions of human beings to do without this fundamental part of their lives solely so that others are not inconvenienced, or in order to comply with a few debatable rules of urbanity? It is not more sensible and less painful to explain to monolingual Americans that to live in places where various living tongues converge can have a certain enriching enchantment, because diversity is also an expression of cultural riches?

But, what is more, American society spends thousands of millions of dollars every year in attempting unavailingly to get high school and college students to learn Spanish, because it is assumed that mastery of a second language benefits the country. If this is the rationale, then why ask the bilingual citizens present in the nation to abandon their use of that other language so covetously sought in educational establishments?

Fear of Spanish and the desire that only English be spoken in the United States do not stand up to a calm analysis of reality. The United States is and will continue to be a fundamentally English-speaking nation, but it is a fortunate fact for the country that there are other languages and other marginal cultures capable of enriching the powerful current of the mainstream. This can be perfectly understood by any American, even a monolingual one, if he is capable of savoring a Mexican taco while listening to the Miami Sound Machine's *Conga* or reading a wonderful story by Isaac Bashevis Singer written in Yiddish—very near the spot where we were berated by the irate old lady in baseball cap and sneakers.

from
Hunger of Memory

Richard Rodriguez

SUPPORTERS of bilingual education today imply that students like me miss a great deal by not being taught in their family's language. What they seem not to recognize is that, as a socially disadvantaged child, I considered Spanish to be a private language. What I needed to learn in school was that I had the right—and the obligation—to speak the public language of *los gringos*. The odd truth is that my first-grade classmates could have become bilingual, in the conventional sense of that word, more easily than I. Had they been taught (as upper-middle-class children are often taught early) a second language like Spanish or French, they could have regarded it simply as that: another public language. In my case such bilingualism could not have been so quickly achieved. What I did not believe was that I could speak a single public language.

Without question, it would have pleased me to hear my teachers address me in Spanish when I entered the classroom. I would have felt much less afraid. I would have trusted them and responded with ease. But I would have delayed—for how long postponed?—having to learn the language of public society. I would have evaded—and for how long could I have afforded to delay?—learning the great lesson of school, that I had a public identity.

Fortunately, my teachers were unsentimental about their responsibility. What they understood was that I needed to speak a public language. So their voices would search me out, asking me questions. Each time I'd hear them, I'd look up in surprise to see a nun's face frowning at me. I'd mumble, not really meaning to answer. The nun would persist. "Richard, stand up. Don't look at the floor. Speak up. Speak to the entire class, not just to me!" But I couldn't believe that the English language was mine to use. (In part, I did not want to believe it.) I continued to mumble. I resisted the teacher's demands. (Did I somehow suspect that once I learned public language my pleasing family life would be changed?) Silent, waiting for the bell to sound, I remained dazed, diffident, afraid.

Because I wrongly imagined that English was intrinsically a public language and Spanish an intrinsically private one, I easily noted the difference between classroom language and the language of home. At school, words were directed to a general audience of listeners. ('Boys and girls.') Words were meaningfully ordered. And the point was not self-expression alone but to make oneself understood by many others. The teacher quizzed: "Boys and girls, why do we use that word in this sentence? Could we think of a better word to use there? Would the sentence change its meaning if the words were differently arranged? And wasn't there a better way of saying much the same thing?" (I couldn't say. I wouldn't even try to say.)

Three months. Five. Half a year passed. Unsmiling, ever watchful, my teachers noted my silence. They began to connect my behavior with the difficult progress my older sister and brother were making. Until one Saturday morning three nuns arrived at the house to talk to our parents. Stiffly, they sat on the blue living room sofa. From the doorway of another room, spying the visitors, I noted the incongruity—the clash of two worlds, the faces and voices of school intruding upon the familiar setting of home. I overheard one voice gently wondering, "Do your children speak only Spanish at home, Mrs. Rodriguez?" While another voice added, "That Richard especially seems so timid and shy."

That Rich-heard!

With great tact the visitors continued, "Is it possible for you and your husband to encourage your children to practice their English when they are home?" Of course, my parents complied. What would they not do for their children's well-being? And how could they have questioned the Church's authority which those women represented? In an instant, they agreed to give up the language (the sounds) that had revealed and accentuated our family's closeness. The moment after the visitors left, the change was observed. *"Ahora, speak to us en inglés,"* my father and mother united to tell us.

At first, it seemed a kind of game. After dinner each night, the family gathered to practice "our" English. (It was still then *inglés,* a language foreign to us, so we felt drawn as strangers to it.) Laughing, we would try to define words we could not pronounce. We played with strange English sounds, often overanglicizing our pronunciations. And we filled the smiling gaps of our sentences with familiar Spanish sounds. But that was cheating, somebody shouted. Everyone laughed. In school, meanwhile, like my brother and sister, I was required to attend a daily tutoring session. I needed a full year of special attention. I also needed my teachers to keep my attention from straying in class by calling out, *Rich-heard*—their English voices slowly prying loose my ties to my other name, its three notes, *Ri-car-do*. Most of all I needed to hear my mother and father speak to me in a moment of seriousness in broken—suddenly heartbreaking—English. The scene was inevitable: One Saturday morning I entered the kitchen where my parents were talking in Spanish. I did not realize that they were talking in Spanish however until, at the moment they saw me, I heard their voices change to speak English. Those *gringo* sounds they uttered startled me. Pushed me away. In that moment of trivial misunderstanding and profound insight, I felt my throat twisted by unsounded grief. I turned quickly and left the room. But I had no place to escape to with Spanish. (The spell was broken.) My brother and sisters were speaking English in another part of the house.

Again and again in the days following, increasingly angry, I was obliged to hear my mother and father: "Speak to us *en inglés.*" *(Speak.)* Only then did I determine to learn classroom English. Weeks after, it happened: One day in school I raised my hand to volunteer an answer. I spoke out in a loud voice. And I did not think it remarkable when the entire class understood. That day, I moved very far from the disadvantaged child I had been only days earlier. The belief, the calming assurance that I belonged in public, had at last taken hold.

Shortly after, I stopped hearing the high and loud sounds of *los gringos*. A more and more confident speaker of English, I didn't trouble to listen to *how* strangers sounded, speaking to me. And there simply were too many English-speaking people in my day for me to hear American accents anymore. Conversations quickened. Listening to persons who sounded eccentrically pitched voices, I usually noted their sounds for an initial few seconds before I concentrated on *what* they were saying. Conversations became content-full. Transparent. Hearing someone's *tone* of voice—angry or questioning or sarcastic or happy or sad—I didn't distinguish it from the words it expressed. Sound and word were thus tightly wedded. At the end of a day, I was often bemused, always relieved, to realize how "silent," though crowded with words, my day in public had been. (This public silence measured and quickened the change in my life.)

At last, seven years old, I came to believe what had been technically true since my birth: I was an American citizen.

But the special feeling of closeness at home was diminished by then. Gone was the desperate, urgent, intense feeling of being at home; rare was the experience of feeling myself individualized by family intimates. We remained a loving family, but one greatly changed. No longer so close; no longer bound tight by the pleasing and troubling knowledge of our public separateness. Neither my older brother nor sister rushed home after school anymore. Nor did I. When I arrived home there would often be neighborhood kids in the house. Or the house would be empty of sounds.

Following the dramatic Americanization of their children, even my parents grew more publicly confident. Especially my mother. She learned the names of all the people on our block. And she decided we needed to have a telephone installed in the house. My father continued to use the word *gringo*. But it was no longer charged with the old bitterness or distrust. (Stripped of any emotional content, the word simply became a name for those Americans not of Hispanic descent.) Hearing him, sometimes, I wasn't sure if he was pronouncing the Spanish word *gringo* or saying gringo in English.

Matching the silence I started hearing in public was a new quiet at home. The family's quiet was partly due to the fact that, as we children learned more and more English, we shared fewer and fewer words with our parents. Sentences needed to be spoken slowly when a child addressed his mother or father. (Often the parent wouldn't understand.) The child would need to repeat himself. (Still the parent misunderstood.) The young voice, frustrated, would end up saying, "Never mind"—the subject was closed. Dinners would be noisy with the clinking of knives and forks against dishes. My mother would smile softly between her remarks; my father at the other end of the table would chew and chew at his food, while he stared over the heads of his children.

My *mother!* My *father!* After English became my primary language, I no longer knew what words to use in addressing my parents. The old Spanish words (those tender accents of sound) I had used earlier—*mamá and papá*—I couldn't use anymore. They would have been too painful reminders of how much had changed in my life. On the other hand, the words I heard neighborhood kids call *their* parents seemed equally unsatisfactory. *Mother* and *Father; Ma, Papa, Pa, Dad, Pop* (how I hated the all-American sound of that last word especially)—all these terms I felt were unsuitable, not really terms of address for *my* parents. As a result, I never used them at home. Whenever I'd speak to my parents, I would try to get their attention with eye contact alone. In public conversations, I'd refer to "my parents" or "my mother and father."

My mother and father, for their part, responded differently, as their children spoke to them less. She grew restless, seemed troubled and anxious at the scarcity of words exchanged in the house. It was she who would question me about my day when I came home from school. She smiled at small talk. She pried at the edges of my sentences to get me to say something more. (What?) She'd join conversations she overheard, but her intrusions often stopped her children's talking. By contrast, my father seemed reconciled to the new quiet. Though his English improved somewhat, he retired into silence. At dinner he spoke very little. One night his children and even his wife helplessly giggled at his garbled English pronunciation of the Catholic Grace before Meals. Thereafter he made his wife recite the prayer at the start of each meal, even on formal occasions, when there were guests in the house. Hers became the public voice of the family. On official business, it was she, not my father, one would usually hear on the phone or in stores, talking to strangers. His children grew so accustomed to his silence that, years later, they would speak routinely of his shyness. (My mother would often try to explain: Both his parents died when he was eight. He was raised by an uncle who treated him like little more than a menial servant. He was never encouraged to speak. He grew up alone. A man of few words.) But my father was not shy, I realized, when I'd watch him speaking Spanish with relatives. Using Spanish, he was quickly effusive. Especially when talking with other men, his voice would spark, flicker, flare alive with sounds. In Spanish, he expressed ideas and feelings he rarely revealed in English. With firm Spanish sounds, he conveyed confidence and authority English would never allow him.

The silence at home, however, was finally more than a literal silence. Fewer words passed between parent and child, but more profound was the silence that resulted from my inattention to sounds. At about the time I no longer bothered to listen with care to the sounds of English in public, I grew careless about listening to the sounds family members made when they spoke. Most of the time I heard someone speaking at home and didn't distinguish his sounds from the words people uttered in public. I didn't even pay much attention to my parents' accented and ungrammatical speech. At least not at home. Only when I was with them in public would I grow alert to their accents. Though, even then, their sounds caused me less and less concern. For I was increasingly confident of my own public identity.

I would have been happier about my public success had I not sometimes recalled what it had been like earlier, when my family had conveyed its intimacy through a set of conveniently private sounds. Sometimes in public, hearing a stranger, I'd hark back to my past. A Mexican farmworker approached me downtown to ask directions to somewhere. *"Hijito . . . ?"* he said. And his voice summoned deep longing. Another time, standing beside my mother in the visiting room of a Carmelite convent, before the dense screen which rendered the nuns shadowy figures, I heard several Spanish-speaking nuns—their busy, singsong overlapping voices—assure us that yes, yes, we were remembered, all our family was remembered in their prayers. (Their voices echoed faraway family sounds.) Another day, a dark-faced old woman— her hand light on my shoulder—steadied herself against me as she boarded a bus. She murmured something I couldn't quite comprehend. Her Spanish voice came near, like the face of a never-before-seen relative in the instant before I was kissed. Her voice, like so many of the Spanish voices I'd hear in public, recalled the golden age of my youth. Hearing Spanish then, I continued to be a careful, if sad, listener to sounds. Hearing a Spanish-speaking family walking behind me, I turned to look. I smiled for an instant, before my glance found the Hispanic-looking faces of strangers in the crowd going by.

Family story for your twenty-first birthday

(con gracias a Alan Pogue por su foto que me inspiro)

Teresa Paloma Acosta

I sit on our bed
And hold you
Wrapped in a blanket.
You are toasty in my arms.
I don't want to let you go.

You are ours now
With your headful
Of softest black hair.
We will take you
With us wherever we wander.
We will carry all your wares
Now that you have claimed another corner
Of the house. No matter what items
Of foolish wonder you collect:
Old tin cans, marbles, dolls.
We'll pack them and unpack them.
Everyone needs a history.

On the bedpost above me
I have pasted pictures
Of Tio Chuy,
Primas hermanas Olivia, Carolina, Antonio, Maria Ignacia.
Of Tia Susana and Tio Chema
And their brood.
All los meros, meros of our family.
We will take their pictures also
Folded snugly in an envelope
Wherever we're sent by
God and the wind.
The vicissitudes of work.

Below at the other end of our bed
Is yours:
A wicker basket,
A white voile/lace curtain atop it.
Inside are soft sheets and blankets
For your tiny body.

The room contained other things
But all I remember
Is you, me, tu papá, la familia.

Shut your eyes now and
You will see them
As plainly as I do.

I have this picture of us on the bed
That day.
Here,
It's yours
Now that you're ready
To be a man.

All that I have to give you
Today are clean and soft white sheets.
All that I have to give you today
Is the curve of my arm
Holding you against my warmth.

Someday I will need to
Be held by your arms:
Crossing streets,
Rising from chairs on
Anniversaries.
El chocolate steaming.

You will let me lean against your strength.

In a Neighborhood in Los Angeles

Francisco X. Alarcón

I learned
Spanish
from my grandma

mijito
don't cry
she'd tell me

on the mornings
my parents
would leave

to work
at the fish
canneries

my grandma
would chat
with chairs

sing them
old
songs

dance
waltzes with them
in the kitchen

when she'd say
niño barrigón
she'd laugh

with my grandma
I learned
to count clouds

to point out
in flowerpots
mint leaves

my grandma
wore moons
on her dress

Mexico's mountains
deserts
ocean

in her eyes
I'd see them
in her braids

I'd touch them
in her voice
smell them

one day
I was told:
she went far away

but still
I feel her
with me

whispering
in my ear
mijito

Which Line Is This? I Forget

Lorna Dee Cervantes

What a fool's game I'm playing,
this foolish game called
"Shame."
Where the rules are rigid
and the stakes are high
and you play for keeps.
Constantly running,
lying,
making up lies to cover my lies,
pretending,
hiding from something I know nothing about.
Talking fast
because I'm not quite sure of what I'm saying.
Feeling close kin to the Ugly Duckling.
Not a turkey
yet
not quite a swan.
Pretending I'm "White"
when they tell me I'm "Mexican."
Pretending I'm "Mexican"
when they tell me I'm "White."

"Hey, Boss Man!"
Wherever you are
in Heaven
or in Hell
I'm not fussy.
I just want someone to tell me which line this is
                              I forget

The Latin Deli: An Ars Poetica

Judith Ortiz Cofer

Presiding over a formica counter,
plastic Mother and Child magnetized
to the top of an ancient register,
the heady mix of smells from the open bins
of dried codfish, the green plantains
hanging in stalks like votive offerings,
she is the Patroness of Exiles,
a woman of no-age who was never pretty,
who spends her days selling canned memories
while listening to the Puerto Ricans complain
that it would be cheaper to fly to San Juan
than to buy a pound of Bustelo coffee here,
and to Cubans perfecting their speech
of a "glorious return" to Havana—where no one
has been allowed to die and nothing to change until then;
to Mexicans who pass through, talking lyrically
of *dólares* to be made in El Norte—
                              all wanting the comfort
of spoken Spanish, to gaze upon the family portrait
of her plain wide face, her ample bosom
resting on her plump arms, her look of maternal interest
as they speak to her and each other
of their dreams and their disillusions—
how she smiles understanding,
when they walk down the narrow aisles of her store
reading the labels of packages aloud, as if
they were the names of lost lovers: *Suspiros,*
Merengues, the stale candy of everyone's childhood.
                              She spends her days
slicing *jamón y queso* and wrapping it in wax paper
tied with string: plain ham and cheese
that would cost less at the A&P, but it would not satisfy
the hunger of the fragile old man lost in the folds
of his winter coat, who brings her lists of items
that he reads to her like poetry, or the others,
whose needs she must divine, conjuring up products
from places that now exist only in their hearts—
closed ports she must trade with.

Tony Went to the Bodega but He Didn't Buy Anything

for Angel Guadalupe

Martín Espada

Tony's father left the family
and the Long Island City projects,
leaving a mongrel-skinny puertorriqueño boy
nine years old
who had to find work.

Makengo the Cuban
let him work at the bodega.
In grocery aisles
he learned the steps of the dry-mop mambo,
banging the cash register
like piano percussion
in the spotlight of Machito's orchestra,
polite with the abuelas who bought on credit,
practicing the grin on customers
he'd seen Makengo grin
with his bad yellow teeth.

Tony left the projects too,
with a scholarship for law school.
But he cursed the cold primavera
in Boston;
the cooking of his neighbors
left no smell in the hallway,
and no one spoke Spanish
(not even the radio).

So Tony walked without a map
through the city,
a landscape of hostile condominiums

and the darkness of white faces,
sidewalk-searcher lost
till he discovered the projects.

Tony went to the bodega
but he didn't buy anything:
he sat by the doorway satisfied
to watch la gente (people
island-brown as him)
crowded in and out,
hablando español,
thought: this is beautiful,
and grinned
his bodega grin.

This is a rice and beans
success story:
today Tony lives on Tremont Street,
above the bodega.

We Live by What
We See at Night

for my father

Martín Espada

When the mountains of Puerto Rico
flickered in your sleep
with a moist green light,
when you saw green bamboo hillsides
before waking to East Harlem rooftops
or Texas barracks,
when you crossed the bridge
built by your grandfather
over a river glimpsed
only in interrupted dreaming,
the craving for that island birthplace
burrowed, deep
as thirty years' exile,
constant as your pulse.

This was the inheritance
of your son, born in New York:
that years before
I saw Puerto Rico,
I saw the mountains
looming above the projects,
overwhelming Brooklyn,
living by what I saw at night,
with my eyes closed.

A Voice

Pat Mora

Even the lights on the stage unrelenting
as the desert sun couldn't hide the other
students, their eyes also unrelenting,
students who spoke English every night

as they ate their meat, potatoes, gravy.
Not you. In your house that smelled like
rose powder, you spoke Spanish formal
as your father, the judge without a courtroom

in the country he floated to in the dark
on a flatbed truck. He walked slow
as a hot river down the narrow hall
of your house. You never dared to race past him

to say, "Please move," in the language
you learned effortlessly, as you learned to run,
the language forbidden at home, though your mother
said you learned it to fight with the neighbors.

You like winning with words. You liked
writing speeches about patriotism and democracy.
You liked all the faces looking at you, all those eyes.
"How did I do it?" you ask me now. "How did I do it

when my parents didn't understand?"
The family story says your voice is the voice
of an aunt in Mexico, spunky as a peacock.
Family stories sing of what lives in the blood.

You told me only once about the time you went
to the state capitol, your family proud as if
you'd been named governor. But when you looked
around, the only Mexican in the auditorium,

you wanted to hide from those strange faces.
Their eyes were pinpricks, and you faked
hoarseness. You, who are never at a loss
for words, felt your breath stick in your throat

like an ice cube. "I can't," you whispered.
"I can't." Yet you did. Not that day but years later.
You taught the four of us to speak up.
This is America, Mom. The undoable is done

in the next generation. Your breath moves
through the family like the wind
moves through the trees.

Immigrants

Pat Mora

wrap their babies in the American flag,
feed them mashed hot dogs and apple pie,
name them Bill and Daisy,
buy them blonde dolls that blink blue
eyes or a football and tiny cleats
before the baby can even walk,
speak to them in thick English,
          hallo, babee, hallo,
whisper in Spanish or Polish
when the babies sleep, whisper
in the dark parent bed, that dark
parent fear, "Will they like
our boy, our girl, our fine american
boy, our fine american girl?"

Elena

Pat Mora

My Spanish isn't enough.
I remember how I'd smile
listening to my little ones,
understanding every word they'd say,
their jokes, their songs, their plots.
    Vamos a pedirle dulces a mamá. Vamos.
But that was in Mexico.
Now my children go to American high schools.
They speak English. At night they sit around
the kitchen table, laugh with one another.
I stand by the stove and feel dumb, alone.
I bought a book to learn English.
My husband frowned, drank more beer.
My oldest said, *"Mamá,* he doesn't want you
to be smarter than he is." I'm forty,
embarrassed at mispronouncing words,
embarrassed at the laughter of my children,
the grocer, the mailman. Sometimes I take
my English book and lock myself in the bathroom,
say the thick words softly,
for if I stop trying, I will be deaf
when my children need my help.

Coffee Bloom

Aurora Levins Morales

In my country
the coffee blooms between hurricanes
fragile white blossoms that a raindrop could trample into
    the mud
a delicacy of lace
a hoax of helplessness smothering up the wiry wood
    within.

On the hillside, deep in the rainforest
is a bush gone wild fifty years ago
its root as thick as my arm.
Here in the green shadows we whisper, the bush and I,
    our secret,
that hidden root
the reason we don't tremble, though the bruised petals
    flail
no matter how wildly the wet winds blows.

Sweet Drama

Luis Omar Salinas

On a night like this . . .
with rain in the distant mountains
soup steaming in the kitchen
my father reads the newspaper
polite, gentle, and at peace
with himself nearing his 80th birthday
There is little in the news
that disturbs him now.
He is happy God has
given him a long life
a woman to love and a son
who knows enough
to walk outside and praise
the olive groves and figs
to whistle along with the sunlight
as they both saunter along
the quiet farming roads . . .

My mother sleeps the sleep of angels
the blue sleep of gardenias touched
by moonlight. Today
she poured orange juice
on her cereal by mistake
she smiled and shook her head—
old age here has the makings
of a sweet drama . . .

Field Poem

Gary Soto

When the foreman whistled
My brother and I
Shouldered our hoes,
Leaving the field.
We returned to the bus
Speaking
In broken English, in broken Spanish
The restaurant food,
The tickets to a dance
We wouldn't buy with our pay.

From the smashed bus window,
I saw the leaves of cotton plants
Like small hands
Waving good-bye.

I Am Offering This Poem

Jimmy Santiago Baca

I am offering this poem to you,
since I have nothing else to give.
Keep it like a warm coat
when winter comes to cover you,
or like a pair of thick socks
the cold cannot bite through,

       I love you,

I have nothing else to give you,
so it is a pot full of yellow corn
to warm your belly in winter,
it is a scarf for your head, to wear
over your hair, to tie up around your face,

       I love you,

Keep it, treasure this as you would
if you were lost, needing direction,
in the wilderness life becomes when mature;
and in the corner of your drawer,
tucked away like a cabin or hogan
in dense trees, come knocking,
and I will answer, give you directions,
and let you warm yourself by this fire,
rest by this fire, and make you feel safe,

       I love you,

It's all I have to give,
and all anyone needs to live,
and to go on living inside,
when the world outside
no longer cares if you live or die;
remember,

       I love you.

All the Fancy Things

William Carlos Williams

music and painting and all that
That's all they thought of
in Puerto Rico in the old Spanish
days when she was a girl

So that now
she doesn't know what to do

with herself alone
and growing old up here—

Green is green
but the tag ends
of older things, *ma chère*

must withstand rebuffs
from that which returns
to the beginnings—

Or what? a
clean air, high up, unoffended
by gross odors

Biographical Notes

Julia Alvarez (born 1950) Born in the Dominican Republic, Alvarez moved to New York City when she was ten. Her experiences adapting to life in the Untied States are often the subject of her writings. She now lives in Vermont, where she writes and teaches.

Sandra Cisneros (born 1954) The publication of *Woman Hollering Creek and Other Stories* (1991) won Cisneros critical acclaim and helped open doors for other Latino writers. Cisneros was born in Chicago into a large Mexican American family. Much of her writing depicts her experiences as a Mexican American woman and the challenges which that presents.

Judith Oritz Cofer (born 1952) Traveling between the physical and cultural borders of Puerto Rico and Paterson, New Jersey, shaped Cofer's unique portrayal of the Latino American experience. Her works include her autobiography, *Silent Dancing: A Partial Remembrance of a Puerto Rican Childhood*, which not only depicts her cultural confusion but also explores the universal pains of growing up. Cofer is also a poet and novelist and teaches at the University of Georgia.

Hugo Martínez-Serros (born 1930) The works of Martínez-Serros capture the challenges and hardships immigrants face in the harsh realities of city life, as well as the joys and triumphs of overcoming such challenges. Many of his stories, such as "Distillation," are based on his experiences growing up in South Chicago of Mexican-born parents. In addition to writing, Martínez-Serros teaches Spanish American literature at Lawrence University in Appleton, Wisconsin.

Nicholasa Mohr (born 1935) This writer is considered by many to be the foremost U.S.-based Puerto Rican writer of her generation. She has received many awards for her writing, including *The New York Times* Outstanding Book of the Year and the American Book Award. Mohr, who sets many of her stories in New York City, lives in Brooklyn, New York.

Rudolfo A. Anaya (born 1937) History concerns Anaya in much of his writing. His first novel, *Bless Me, Ultima* (1972), won national acclaim for its moving depiction of the culture and history of

New Mexico. Teaming with José Griego y Maestas, Anaya brings the Latino heritage to a larger audience by retelling Spanish *cuentos,* or folk tales, in English.

José Griego y Maestas (born 1949) This language education expert lives in Santa Fe, New Mexico. He has adapted many oral Spanish tales, or *cuentos,* into written Spanish. Working with Rudolfo A. Anaya, who translates the tales into English, they have brought the oral traditions of Spanish-speaking peoples to a larger audience.

Ricardo E. Alegría (born 1921) The influence of Alegría's professional background as an anthropologist and historian are evident in his passion for collecting folk tales rich in the history of Puerto Rico. He is a professor of history at the University of Puerto Rico and has served as the director of the Institute of Puerto Rican Culture and the Archaeological Museum and Research Center at the University of Puerto Rico.

Esmeralda Santiago (born 1948) The eldest of eleven children, Santiago moved to New York City from Puerto Rico in 1961. Her autobiography, *When I Was Puerto Rican,* explores her confusion that resulted from feeling like an outsider in her native country but not feeling one hundred percent American. She is now a journalist and jointly owns a film company with her husband.

Gary Soto (born 1952) Award-winning poet, storyteller, and nonfiction writer Soto draws upon his working-class Mexican American background and experiences growing up in Fresno, California, when creating his works. Soto teaches Chicano Studies and English at the University of California at Berkeley.

Carlos Alberto Montaner (born 1943) To escape a prison sentence for protesting Castro's policies, Montaner fled Cuba and came to the United States in 1961. In 1970, he moved to Madrid, Spain, and established a publishing house; he also publishes a weekly column that appears in most of the Spanish newspapers in the world.

Richard Rodriguez (born 1944) The author's highly regarded autobiography, *Hunger of Memory: The Education of Richard Rodriguez,* tells how he came to learn English from the Catholic nuns who taught in the school he attended. Rodriguez is an editor at Pacific News Service in Los Angeles, as well as a contributing editor to *Harper's* and the *Los Angeles Times*.

Teresa Paloma Acosta (born 1949) Acosta often uses her poetry to record and celebrate both her family history and her Hispanic heritage. As a child, she enjoyed the stories her grandfather would share about his boyhood in Mexico and life as a cowboy. These stories inspired her to begin reading literature and writing poetry.

Francisco X. Alarcón (born 1954) As a child, Alarcón moved between the United States and Mexico, getting his education in two countries and becoming proficient in two languages. His grandfather, a Tarascan Indian, sparked his imagination and interest in writing by telling him stories about Ancient Mexico. Alarcón has written several books of poetry and is a professor at the University of California at Santa Cruz.

Lorna Dee Cervantes (born 1954) California native Cervantes has been writing poetry since she was eight years old. A descendant of the Spanish families who first settled California, she is a committed feminist and Hispanic rights activist. Her establishment of the literary magazine *Mango*, to help nurture other Hispanic writers, serves as evidence of her commitment. Cervantes teaches poetry at the University of Colorado.

Martín Espada (born 1957) Not many lawyers pursue simultaneous careers as poets, but Espada was—until 1993—an exception. He now teaches writing at the University of Massachusetts at Amherst and continues to write poetry that reflects his Puerto Rican background.

Pat Mora (born 1942) Mora was born and raised in El Paso, Texas, near the border that separates Mexico and the United States. Her writing depicts her appreciation of her cultural background and pride in her heritage, as well as the harmony she sees between Mexico and the United States. She has taught at various high schools and universities.

Aurora Levins Morales (born 1954) Morales is the daughter of a Jewish American father and a Puerto Rican mother. Her parents are both anti-war activists, and, as a result, the poet says she was raised on "books and social justice." Morales began writing at the age of seven. Her works examine and embrace her Puerto Rican, Jewish, and mainstream American heritages.

Luis Omar Salinas (born 1937) Salinas knew from a young age that he wanted to be a writer. After completing high school, he worked at odd jobs while attending several California colleges to help accomplish his goal. He is the author of seven books of poetry and the recipient of numerous awards. In addition to being an accomplished writer, Salinas works as a Spanish translator.

Jimmy Santiago Baca (born 1952) Born in New Mexico, Baca is of Mexican American and Apache ancestry. Baca taught himself to read and write at age eighteen and is now the author of five books of poetry, essays, a screenplay, and a novel. He lives in Albuquerque, New Mexico.

William Carlos Williams (1883–1963) Williams grew up in a Spanish-speaking home in Paterson, New Jersey. His mother was Puerto Rican and his father of English-Caribbean descent. Williams pursued a duel career as a poet and a pediatrician. His poetry focuses on the essence of modern American life by depicting daily life in everyday language. Williams's vision of America was also influenced by growing up in a bilingual, bicultural home, and much of his poetry reflects the influences of his Latino upbringing.

Acknowledgments *(continued from p. ii)*

Susan Bergholz Literary Services

"Only Daughter" by Sandra Cisneros. Copyright © 1990 by Sandra Cisneros. First published in GLAMOUR November 1990. All rights reserved. "Geraldo: No Last Name" by Sandra Cisneros, from *The House on Mango Street*. Copyright © 1989 by Sandra Cisneros. Originally published, in somewhat different form, by Arte Publico Press in 1984 and revised in 1989. Published by Vintage Books, a division of Random House, Inc., New York, and in hard cover by Alfred A. Knopf. All rights reserved. "Daughter of Invention" from *How the Garcia Girls Lost Their Accents* by Julia Alvarez. Copyright © 1991 by Julia Alvarez. Published by Plume, an imprint of New American Library, a division of Penguin Books USA; originally published in hardcover by Algonquin Books of Chapel Hill. Reprinted by permission of Susan Bergholz Literary Services, New York. All rights reserved.

Bilingual Press/Editorial Bilingüe

"Tony Went to the Bodega but He Didn't Buy Anything" and "We Live by What We See at Night" by Martín Espada, from *Trumpets from the Islands of their Eviction*. Copyright © 1987 Bilingual Press/Editorial Bilingüe. Reprinted by permission of Bilingual Press/Editorial Bilingüe, Arizona State University, Tempe, AZ.

Chronicle Books

"In a Neighborhood in Los Angeles" by Francisco X. Alarcón. Copyright © 1990 by Francisco Alarcón.

Firebrand Books

"Coffee Bloom" by Aurora Levins Morales, from *Getting Home Alive* by Aurora Levins Morales and Rosario Morales. Copyright © 1986 Aurora Levins Morales.

David R. Godine, Publisher, Inc.

From *Hunger of Memory: The Education of Richard Rodriguez*, an autobiography. Copyright © 1982 by Richard Rodriguez. Used by permission of David R. Godine, Publisher, Inc.

Harcourt Brace & Company

"Lazy Peter and His Three-Cornered Hat" from *The Three Wishes: A Collection of Puerto Rican Folktales*, Selected and adapted by Ricardo E. Alegría, translated by Elizabeth Culbert. Copyright © 1969 by Ricardo E. Alegría.

HarperCollins Publishers Inc.

"Mr. Mendelsohn" from *El Bronx Remembered: A Novella and Stories* by Nicholasa Mohr. Copyright © 1975 by Nicholasa Mohr.

Carlos A. Montaner

"Why Fear Spanish?" by Carlos A. Montaner, from *Miami Herald*, April 25, 1988. Reprinted by permission of the author.

Museum of New Mexico Press

"The Lost Camel" ("El camello que se perdio") and "The Force of Luck" ("La suerte") from *Cuentos: Tales from the Hispanic Southwest*, Spanish and English, by Jose Griego y Maestas and Rudolfo A. Anaya. Copyright © by The Museum of New Mexico Press.

New Directions Publishing Corporation

"I Am Offering This Poem" from *Immigrants in Our Own Land & Selected Early Poems* by Jimmy Santiago Baca. Copyright © 1982 by Jimmy Santiago Baca. "All the Fancy Things" by William Carlos Williams from *The Collected Poems of William Carlos Williams*, Volume I 1909-1939, edited by A. Walton Litz and Christopher MacGowan. Copyright © 1986 by A. Walton Litz and Christopher MacGowan.

Acknowledgments